Are you looking for me? Look on.
    You won't find me.
    Because I'm dancing,
    Dancing to the thunder of indescribable
    Rhythm.

JAZZ WOMEN SOUL

Poems of a Black Musician

Jim Marks

CELESTIAL ARTS
Millbrae, California

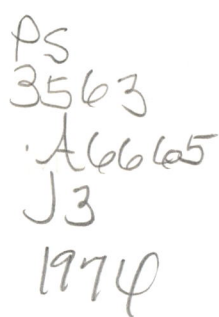

Copyright©1974 by Celestial Arts
231 Adrian Road, Millbrae, California 94030

No part of this book may be reproduced by any mechanical, photographic, or electronic process, or in the form of a phonographic recording, nor may it be stored in a retrieval system, transmitted, or otherwise copied for public or private use without the written permission of the publisher.

First Printing, July 1974
Printed in the United States of America

Library of Congress Cataloging in Publication Data

Marks, Jim, 1934 -
    Jazz, women, soul.

      Poems.
        I. Title.
PS3563.A6665J3   811'.5'4   74-8321
ISBN 0-912310-71-5

AN INTRODUCTION

Jim Marks' poems are written to be sounded, written to be spoken, moaned, groaned, shouted, screamed, whispered, sung, even danced to as the spirit calls for.

Unlike many poets writing today, Marks is solidly grounded in song. When I first had the pleasure of being exposed to his talent, he was earning his living playing black classical music; a drummer whose love of rhythm and melody must have been so overwhelming that it burned to take wing and seek expression in other forms. Fittingly enough, poetry turns out to have been the direction in which it was headed.

Whether he's celebrating or musing on woman in all her many aspects, children, oceans, daylight, night, struggle, bridges, color, astronauts, drugs, prison or inner serenity, the presence of music can always be felt in the language he plays.

Beethoven, Louis Armstrong, Billie Holiday, Charlie Parker, Miles Davis, Thelonious Monk, John Coltrane, Jimi Hendrix—Marks gets down and addresses them all "face to face, mouth to mouth" in what he so aptly terms "ear time." The phrase to me vividly evokes the flavor of those transcendental moments which we all experience at one time or another as we abandon our physical bodies and all that passes for reality to suddenly find ourselves tuned in to voicings that the secret heart alone dictates. "Like touching the nerve endings of space," is the way the poet perceives it.

Ah, the man's exuberance and yea-saying affirmation and love of life itself, for all its pleasure and pain! This is what comes across in these poems. Angel and demon, gospel and blues — the spiritual and the sensual, like sunlight and shadow, blend with one another here in a way that's dramatically engaging.

Poet Jim Marks is one of those rare birds perfectly capable of enduring life's slightings, rude assaults and disappointments without losing sight of the light.

Al Young

DEDICATION

To my beautiful wife, Jeanene,
who helped me create by loving me
and
To my grandmother, Caroline Marks,
who left a spirit in my heart.

JAZZ

... most of me is what
I'm doing ...
read about it.

PEACE

PEACE	is here every season.
PEACE	has a quiet, beautiful reason.
PEACE	for the help of every man.
PEACE	begins in the heart, not in the hand.
PEACE	can change sorrow to a tender love.
PEACE	must begin right here, before above.
PEACE	can be quiet. Happiness can be quick.
PEACE	can enter the mind that is sick.
PEACE	is freedom and seeing beautiful things.
PEACE	is children playing in the Spring.
PEACE	is not having to knock on a closed door.
PEACE	is sharing NOW. War no more.

I FEEL THE SOUNDS OF RHYTHM

One day I saw
A blackbird flying
    And singing.
Blackbirds all got rhythm.

He had an enchanted swing
    In his body.
He even talked to the wind
    About the sounds of rhythm.

I felt him catching the heart
    Of the sky
He sang from the darkness
Sometimes pretending not to be around,
    Flowing rhythm around the overcrowded
    Earth.

He hid behind the moon once
And drew the vision of wisdom,
Flipped his wings like chickens
    Boogie-wooging.

One morning he flew in my window
    Sitting echoless
Overburdened with loneliness
But in a pleasant way.
    I felt his tired body
He was suggesting
I take his rhythm.

Because he had heard the angels
Whispering,
From the morning sun
He was headed for the town
    Of Bethlehem
Because God was looking
    Down, smiling.
I took his wings and flew away
As I parted the wind
I could feel the sounds
    Of his rhythm.

I OUGHT TO WATCH THAT (EGO)

I am forever trying to tell somebody
    WHO I AM.
I am gettin' kinda tired
    Of explainin'

But only one more time
    I will attempt to persuade,
Risking the danger of not being in
    Harmony with your ear. . .
And maybe I ought to watch that.

When I was just a kid, I married my soul
    And my body became the best man.
I fought the world, and every man knew
    They were in a battle.
Now the depths have enlarged my tongue.

I created a Holy City, walked many days
    And nights in the path of loneliness.
Listened in a silent way to
    Filles de Kilimanjaro.

I froze Captain Zero and made
    His tongue explode.
I drew wisdom from Einstein and Karl Marx
    And injected it into Andy Gump.

I danced in the shadows and grew
    An Afro hairdo on a baldheaded man,
Turned Bossa Nova into Rock and taught
    Brazilians how to play it.

Now, maybe I should raise your hand
    And bless it with gold
Before you can see the
    Hot rhythms of magic in my soul.
Really, I ought to watch that.

FOR POPS

Yes, Pops Satchmo King,
Ambassador of jazz.
    And you and New Orleans,
    You came spreading the gospel of jazz
    Overnight saints that never marched,
    But flashed brightly on Perdido Street
    Where jazz was born.

You heard the trumpets cry.
The smoothness made existence sweeter.
    Then you also cried,
    Because you never heard the sea.
    Only pain and joy
    From cats hollering from across Ramparts Street.
    Yelling about blues, pain, ugliness, and magic.
    And you were melody.

A new pop and
Kid Ory and Joe "King" Oliver,
    Black flannel trousers,
    Statues of heroes.
    And you dedicated your colored quartet
    To the white world.
    Crying, screaming voices from spirits singing.

Yes, it was memories about the
Johns for the colored,
>   And the johns for the whites.
>   Even the back door for the blacks
>   En route to separation.
>   Then you smiled and humored.
>   Your hardest gig was with the loom of
>   Racism and evil in your birth place, New Orleans.

Then, the Promised Land,
But no "In God We Trust."
>   St. Louis and then Kansas City,
>   Chicago, New York, and then your tunes.
>   "Everyday's a Holiday," but no holiday for you.
>   "Swing That Music"
>   "The Skeleton in the Closet"
>   "Struttin' With Some Barbecue"
>   "Your're a Lucky Guy"
>   "Hey, Lawdy Mama"
>   "I Double Dare You"
>   "Thanks a Million"

They are your salvation
Because you fathered them,
>   The spirits of the earth.
>   And there were no "pennies from heaven"
>   Only Pop Foster swinging,
>   And no hotels for niggers.
>   You grinned and jammed, embarrassed,
>   But you grinned.

And there was joy, too.
Like hours of story telling
> With Earl Hines, Benny Goodman, Hamp,
> Count, Duke, Dexter Gordon, Buddy Rich,
> And Lucille, who always had the water hot
> For your morning blues.

Now, Pops, you are with the
Giants of jazz and blues.
> And even if the saints don't march in,
> You can say to Bird, Billie Holiday, Wes,
> Chick Webb, and Jelly Roll Morton,
> "HELLO, DOLLY."

So, Gabriel move over for Pops,
> Let him blow his horn,
> And we shall all be free.

FOR STYLISTIC CHANGES
for John Coltrane

Are you willing to earn?
Are you willing to learn
The music brother John Coltrane
Left here for us to play?
Lyrical, sentimental fashions,
Full of speech-like tones,
The endless flurries of notes he played.

Only Miles Davis comes to mind
When I think of Coltrane's transition.
A beautiful lust, as a poem of love,
But physical and emotional as pain.
Can we listen to the melodious line?

Coltrane's announcement of freedom
Notes plugging as the music floats
Screaming against the charts of your eardrums
But softly as the fresh wind.
Can you witness?
As his music will never die
There will only be extensions
For us to play.

MONTEREY JAZZ FESTIVAL 1970

Thirty thousand costumes
Of every color, transplanting
Faces with styles of their own.
Happy looks in their eyes
As the sun lifts up the world.

And races mixed, while some
Southerner feels he should've
Stayed at home.
Somewhere in the sky, shadows project
Memories and echoes of a delightful generation.

The thirteenth year of a romance, intrigued
By love of life and beauty.
Festival talk, as pot smokers
Never hide their smoke.
World travelers rap about Bird, Diz, and Miles,
Then a cool hipster smiles under his beard.

Twenty-six booths a circle forming,
Paintings, phantom women,
Imported Mexican leather,
And beckoning traders.

Pop, bebop, haunting electric melodies,
Bumpers burning like an eclipse
Fine women in sunglasses,
Silhouetting traffic, noise from radios and tapes.
Bodies touching freely, firecracker dreams,
Images portrayed solely for a weekend.

Oldtimers, blues, and funk
Took over Saturday afternoon.
When all the old timers came up
From the dead ,
Some from the grave, only to return,
Hoping to find a new imagination.

JAZZ IS OURSELVES

JAZZ is the music of the world.
JAZZ is not written—Composers know that, Singers
know that, Players know that, Bands know that.

JAZZ in an arm, JAZZ in a toe, JAZZ in a heart,
JAZZ in a mouth, JAZZ in a foot, JAZZ in a head,
JAZZ in a soul-warm vibration, JAZZ in a sound.

Blow, blow Diz, spirit inspiration of jazz inspires
your mind;
Sing, Ella; swing Duke (It don't mean a thing if it
ain't got that swing!);
Blow, Miles, the dark prince of jazz, and Chick Webb
had the rhythm,
Buddy Rich, Jo Jones played boogie woogie, and that's
jazz.

Diz and brother Parker is bebop,
Parker is dead, jazz lives (jazz is ourselves),
JAZZ is colorless, JAZZ is paying your dues,
Trane dead, Wes dead—Windy, Afro Blue, Love Supreme.

JAZZ is not dope, JAZZ is ourselves,
Help us play the music of the world,
JAZZ eat, JAZZ sleep, JAZZ play, JAZZ lives,
JAZZ is the music of the world.

Beethoven played jazz, and Coleman Hawkins blew until
he was sixty-two,
America adopted a daddy, Louis Armstrong,
JAZZ is ourselves.
White Dixieland player plays jazz in New Orleans,
Benny Goodman blew in Russia.

JAZZ ain't dead, JAZZ is art, JAZZ is the coolness,
ain't that it, the coolness?

JAZZ is ourselves.
It's what the artist is playing or not playing,
It's what the listener is hearing or not hearing:
Bitches brew, in a silent way,
And Gene Ammons plays slow, and Herbie Mann,
Freddie Hubbard, J. J. Johnson, Jimmy Smith,
Thelonious Monk.
JAZZ is not inferior.

JAZZ is listening or not listening.
JAZZ is the music of the world.

POEM FOR JIMI HENDRIX

Your electric guitar
May never play at Woodstock again
But your music will long be in
The ears like purple haze.

Your hair doesn't cover
The nameless gracefulness
Of your sound.
A sound that rocked against
The wind.

Like a love cry, seventeen
Miles away
As we could feel we are alive
And all the generations
Will pick up where you left off.

As you may join brother Otis Redding
You have left "The Electric Ladyland"
In the "Band of Gypsies."

EULOGY FOR DEWEY

And oh, I remembered
Voices drifting,
Then echoing like birds singing.
Shaped in blues and jazz.
Clutching time . . . .
        Rhythm freeing bodies
        From magic and moon.

Oh, and spiritual minds
Living in blues.
Jazz lovers living in mushroom clouds,
Dreaming of sleeping, dark skies,
Miles away from grinding stars.
        When bebop memories and sadass poets
        Become yesterday's world.

We may read new poems,
Poems of wisdom,
New as Miles' protruding wisdom
Of Bird and Lester.
Beyond this planet, they blew love,
   And voices into the earth.
   I remembered Bird,
   And Moody and Diz knew him
   As many fainting substances took him
   And a million mornings went along.

And, oh, Dewey!
You, too, are with the Kings and Queens
Of jazz and inventions.
   And Billie Holiday mourned
   Memories of music and morning blues.

Nights blowing, and shooting smack.
I knew all of it, Dewey.
The moans and screams,
Waiting for the white ghost,
Shaped like a real person.

Oh, and the secret love songs of unchained fire,
Casting dark shadows, smokey paintings
        Of jazz on the walls.
        And oh, the Goddamn rent!

Oh, I tried, Dewey,
But it was too late for you.
It was the last fix, Dewey,
The last fix that did it.
Or maybe the fix before that.

We had long conversations only
Two days before it happened.
Remember, Dewey?
We rapped about dirty needles
And Billie. We rapped about O.D.'s,
Yeah, O.D.'s, Dewey.
        The aching truth,
        The yelling upstairs,
        The greasy spoons,
        And dirty floors.
        The unwiped tables,
        The smell after the rain.

And, oh, the bitch who wouldn't surrender
The night we both wanted sex.
The murderer killed.
I hope they catch him, Dewey,
Before he kills again.

Oh, yes, Archie kicked.
You remember Archie?
The pale nights looking for smack.
He lived down the hall. We sure played some
Wild sounds together. You and me.
Everything is so essential now, Dewey.
Life is everything.
> Life-giving stories, and
> Stories giving life.
Oh, yes, Dewey — I kicked.

THE FESTIVAL

The bands all play
    As a poet writes
A meaningful poem,
    A hidden fold of hipness.
A proud photographer floats
    For a better look at a pink-faced
Fan thumbing through a poetry book.

And the goers to Big Sur still dream
    While redwood trees fall,
As do-gooders shout
    About the rock music in the hall.
But the Festival is across town
    As young people are put down
Because dinkie-doodle eyeballers
    Aren't hip to the new sound.
They sit in mushroom clouds,
    They reappear, as their eyes turn
To look for a juvenile delinquent,
    As their burning philosophies
And emotions drive them home.

Now, Coltrane's music still lives,
    And Miles Davis still gives.
I hear rock in jazz tones,
    Shoeless bars, asses sway
As the rock drummer searches for the right time.
    Music played from the head,
Created by the dead.
    Stereophonic, everything played fast,
The air smells of grass,
    Grasping for breath, chanting,
Screaming, screaming.

Stand full of crowed sunglasses
    Funky bodies, evicted girls
Passing around joints.
    Music floods, crazy beauty,
Some party whores, we love them, too.
    Lovers playing with each other.
I see people, and people
    Who would be people
If they would uncover
    Their minds.

I see people, and people
    In all shades.
I see a mother learning about her
    Daughter for the first time,
And didn't know what to do.
    I see hip people, but I don't see you.

WHERE JAZZ GOES

Yes, I added a little jazz
    To my distance.
Jazz blew through the thin trees
    Of the expensive forest.

I ran to tell the world
    As this music drove deep wedges
Into my flesh.
    Sounds screaming over the blue horizon
Where birds go.

Where birds go, music goes,
    Motion and flesh, where texture is born.
Blues and butterfingers,
    Birds and peacocks.
The streetlamps burn dim
    Over the rented earth.

Sunday mornings after the gigs,
    The town is quiet.
Music and morning blues,
    Come back, jazz. Add more
Distance to my world.
    Stay in my bleeding space.

BAAAAD NEWS FOR MR. BLUES

Good-bye, Mr. Blues
With stretch stockings
And your generated news.
You have been a disease,
Leaving my mind confused,
It's farewell announcing your name.
Yes, I've had some
So I know darn well
Where you're coming from.
I don't seem to need you anymore,
Things have changed.
They're not the same as before.
Go away, Mr. Blues,
I had a mental revolution
You only needed an outlet
And I don't take
Kindly to that.
You used me, and got me strung out
But . . . .oh, Mr. Blues,
I found out what pain was all about.
Go run your game
On a funny brain
Like the ocean who's running
From the Red Sea
I can't use you
And you don't need me.
You are a pimp—
Pimped my mind.

You laid bad dreams
On me last night.
Go away, Mr. Blues,
Get inside your position
Because I have made
A transition.
You remolded my body
Put my head in the sand
Had me checking the zodiac sign
To find out if I was a real man.
You know, Mr. Blues,
Like dead roots don't grow underground—
Walk on.
Your vibes in my ear make a dead sound
On my subconscious awareness.

My resources are concerned
There is no way I can tell you
The things I have learned
Like the darkness that outlasted
The light.
Fool blues ain't no news
I got my sight.

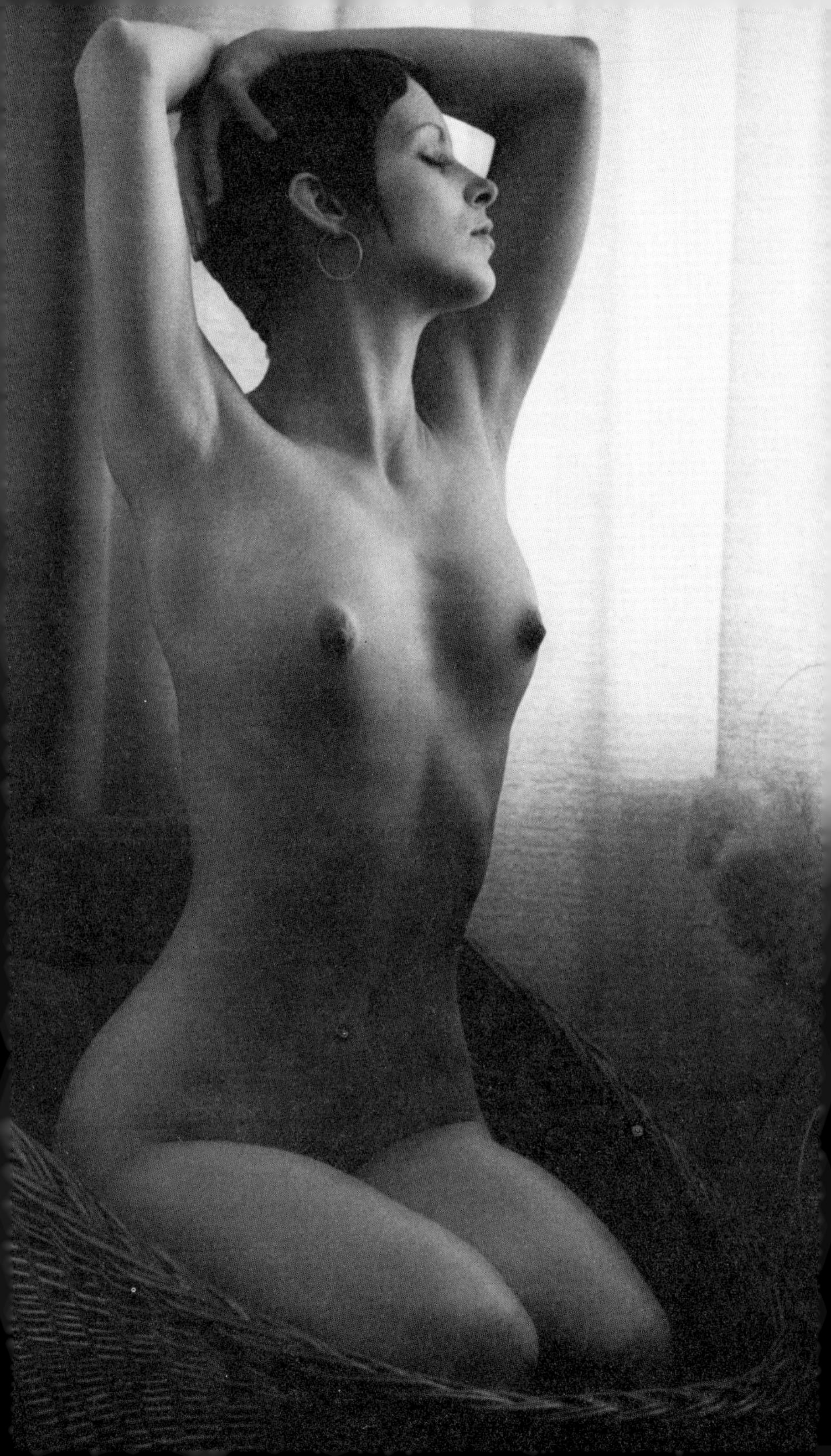

WOMEN

... nothing is so soft
as a naked
      woman.
Her BEAUTY forms
with gentleness
bouncing off the light
of darkness . . . .

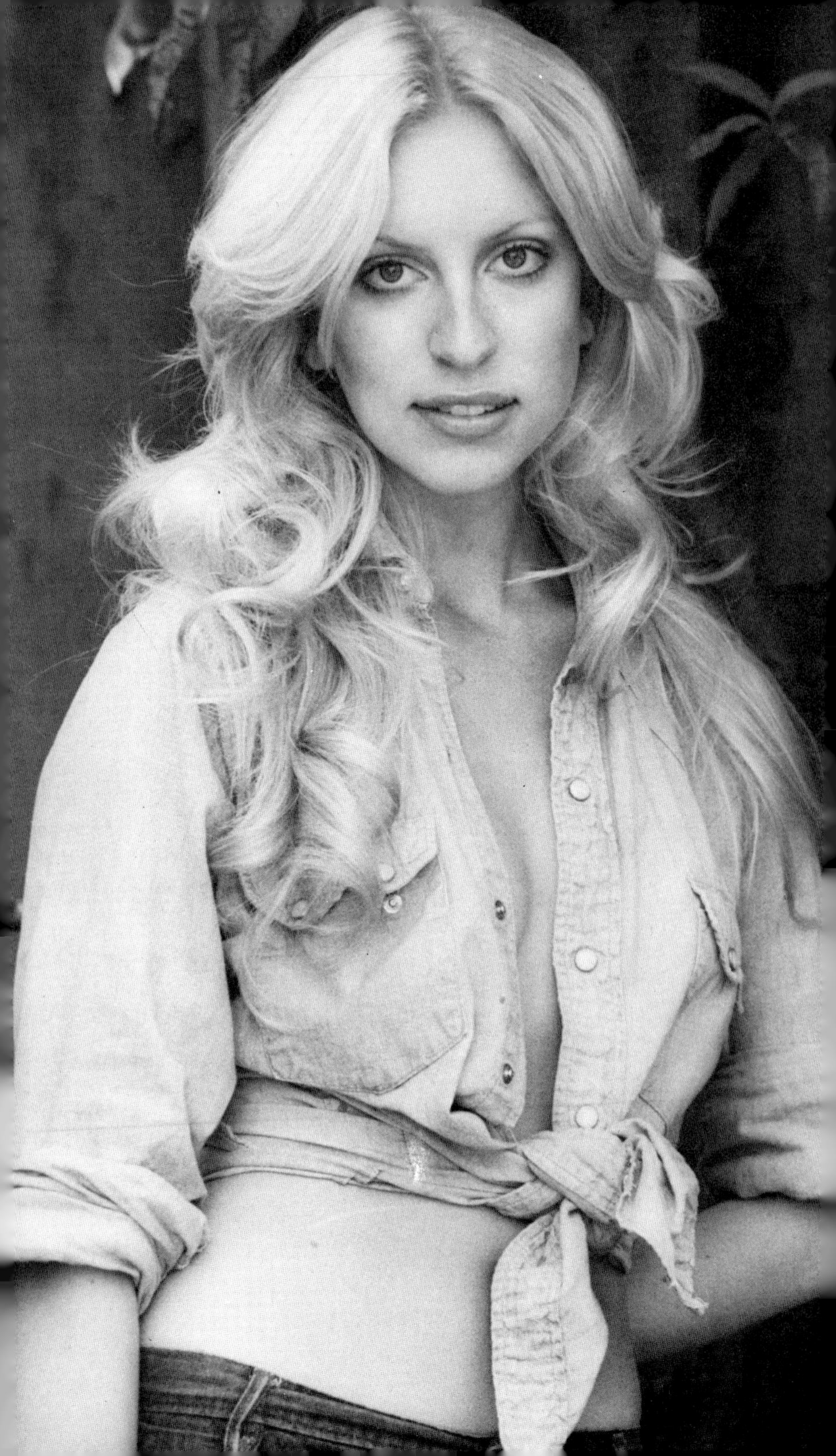

EXTENDED LOVE

I have loved you
A long time before.
I was quiet,
As some in love are,
In love with love, the most tender kind.

I spoke to you one day
On an elevator,
Wing tips beneath the sky
Where the bird sings.
There was a star shining down,
Sparkling everywhere.

I knew a great secret,
You passed before I could speak
An eloquent chill within a dream.
In that dream, there was music
Voices repeating out of twilight.

I will extrovert my love
As a bee extroverts his love for honey
And the birds can sing about it.
I will love you forever,
Because I have loved you
For a long, long time before.

PORTRAIT OF A BLACK WOMAN
for Regina

Not a whisper,
   or sigh,
From a woman
   who moves
Beside her man.

To be his artery,
   and vein,
Who smoothes his
   muscles
When they become
   strained.

She lets the
   morning seeds
Grow and twists
   them into little
Black features.

She knows she
   must clutch a
Disciplined flutter,
   then turn it
Into softness to
   waylay fear.

As the portrait
   grows, nobody
But her Man knows the
   dimensions in
Which nature introduced
   her to him.

She speaks as
   low as
Leaves falling
   from a hilltop,
Lying quietly in a
   fashionable
Shade of darkness.

She need not
   proclaim
Herself a silver
   star or
Queen of Bliss,
   because she has
Created the Portrait
   of a Black Woman.
For her man, she
   blesses, far beyond
Recesses.

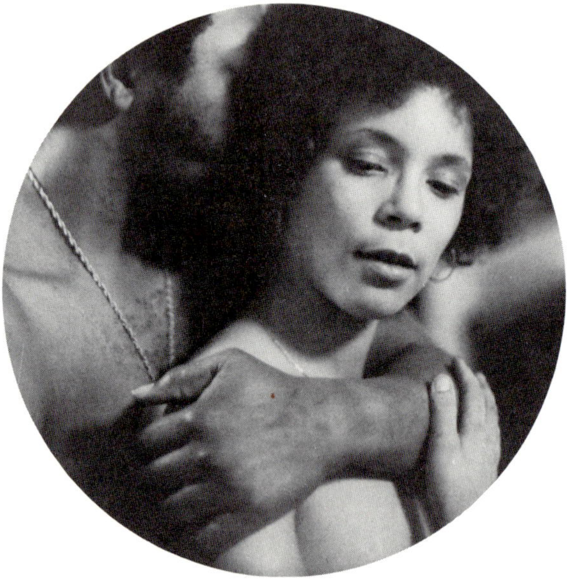

TOUCHING YOUR FEELINGS

I'm trying to touch your love,
Move it out of the sun.
We must find out if the fidelity
Will continue to shine.

I'm trying to touch your feelings
The way I touch your hand.
Because you have grown inside me.
And I feel a bit anxious to circulate
The things I have found out about you.
I'm trying to touch that one moment
That can keep us into natural life
Help me cope with the feeling I'm into.

I'm trying to touch the serenade of your love cries
While listening to velvet music,
As your ripping fingers rip at my flesh.
And when it's time, we gotta-go-on and get
What we got.
My ego is the final analysis of my image
I want to go down and rise in a castle, I must
Bring you along for light.

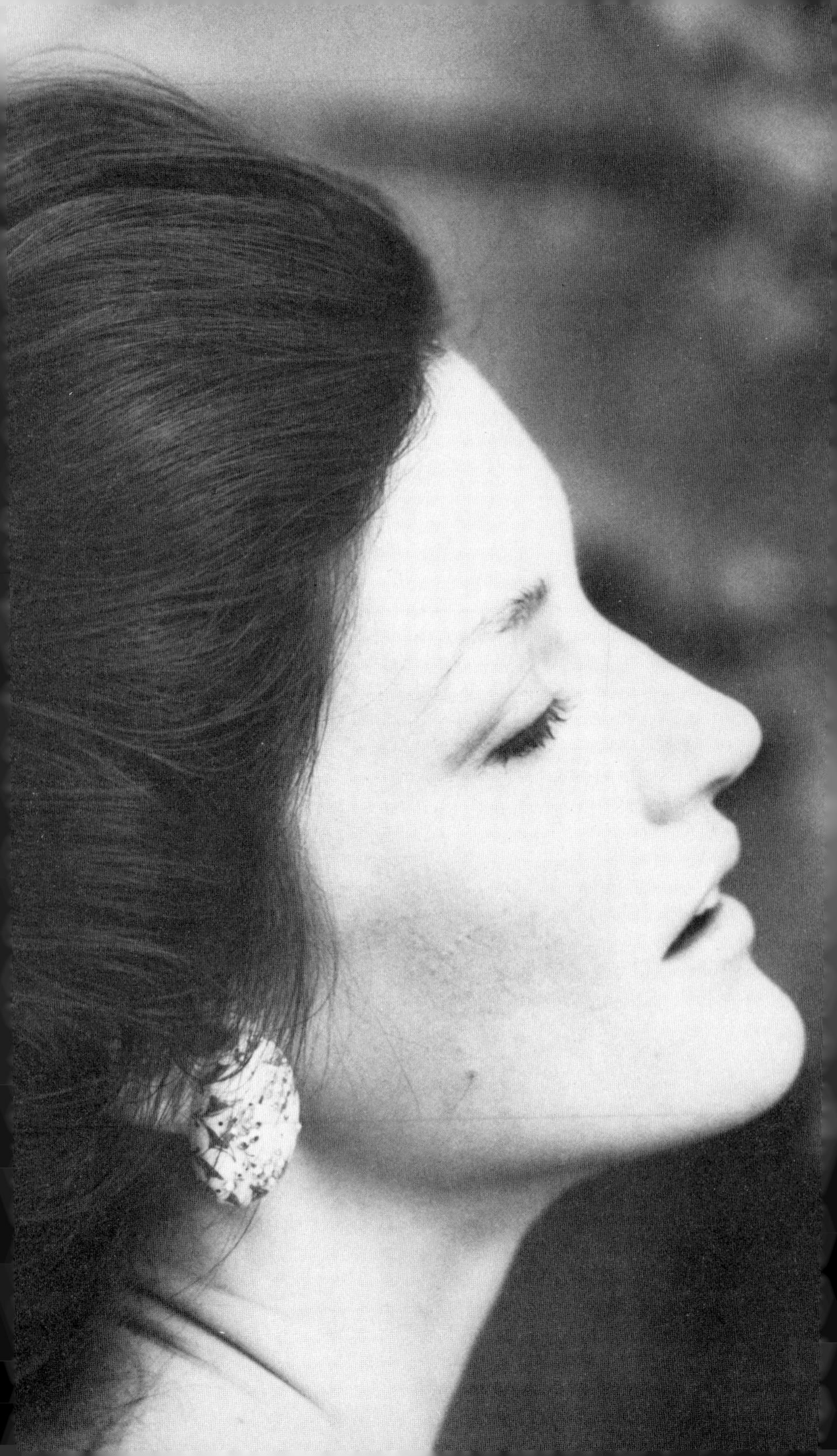

I'm trying to touch you,
Like touching the nerve endings of space.
I'm trying to grow beyond the hanging moon.
I'm trying to touch the nearest spirit.
I'm trying to touch your ultra-beauty
That sings me to sleep at night.
I'm trying to be the articulator
In your dreams, twist shadows into April
Smiles and May mornings into granulated mist.

From here it feels like a melted togetherness.
I'm trying to be inside your flesh
To extend awareness,
And feel the dampness of your
Tears on my shoulder.
I'm trying to touch time.

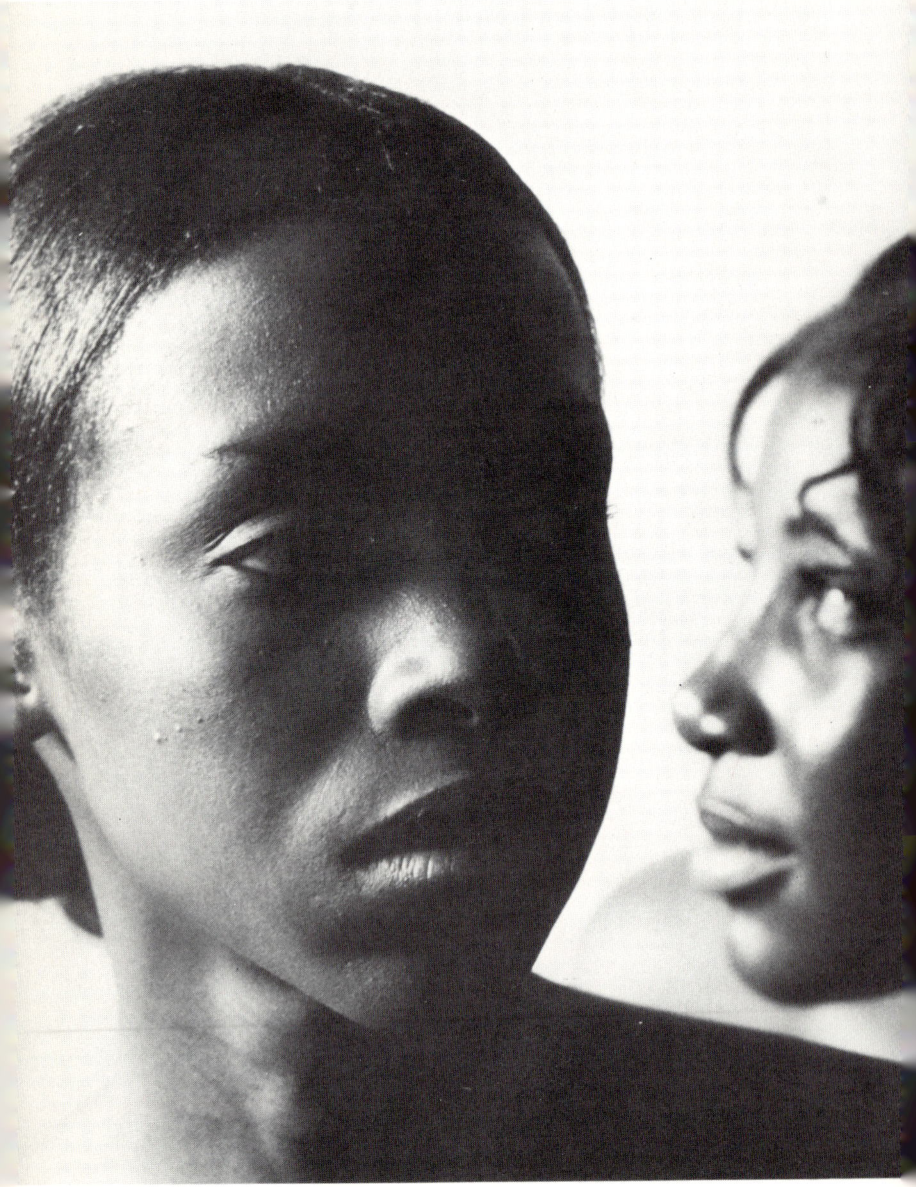

YOU GOTTA HAVE YOUR HEART ON FIRE
for Cherita

Dance the invisible dance
Don't be afraid of what the atmosphere
Is creating for you
Travel through the sky
You gotta have your heart on fire

Snap your finger, turn your thumb inward
Before you sing
You must build a mission for those
Who want to see your beautiful face
Keep an urge to be like a butterfly
You gotta have your heart on fire

Move like the river
Keep the light shining in your eyes
Look for the middle of nowhere
Some will never see you try
But you
Gotta have your heart on fire.

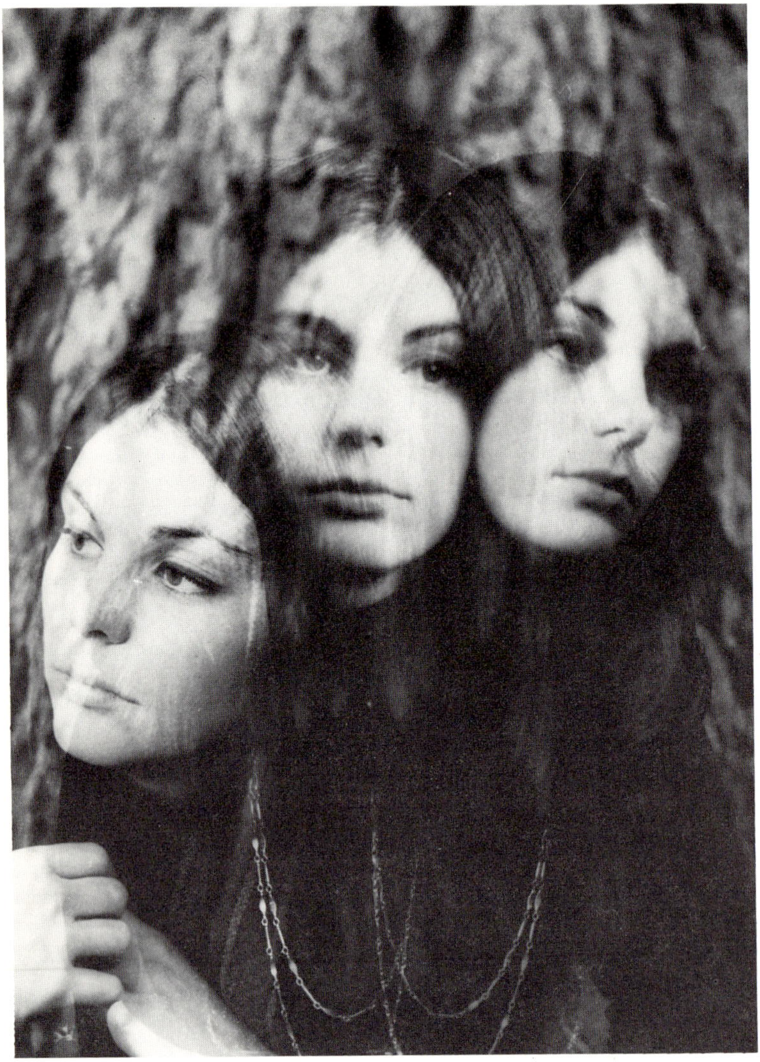

PRIDE TOOK THE BEST

My friend gone
Pudding whipped face
Or falsely rage
Head hanging low
Bursting behind a brash
Ass dragging, out-of-shape
Trail hidden to the very pity of time
Disconnected, paralyzed mind
From dropped down butt
The sheets were the King
Pillows had your head high.
Pride wouldn't let you rest.

Face to face, mouth to mouth
Or ear time
Time for story telling
Tales of beauty
Depths rainbow lust
Lukewarm fire
Circle with cool breeze, aching back.
Pride wouldn't let you rest.

Tonight no longer belongs to you
But tonight, sweetheart, will be crying for lovers
Doing what lovers do best.
Pride would let you rest.

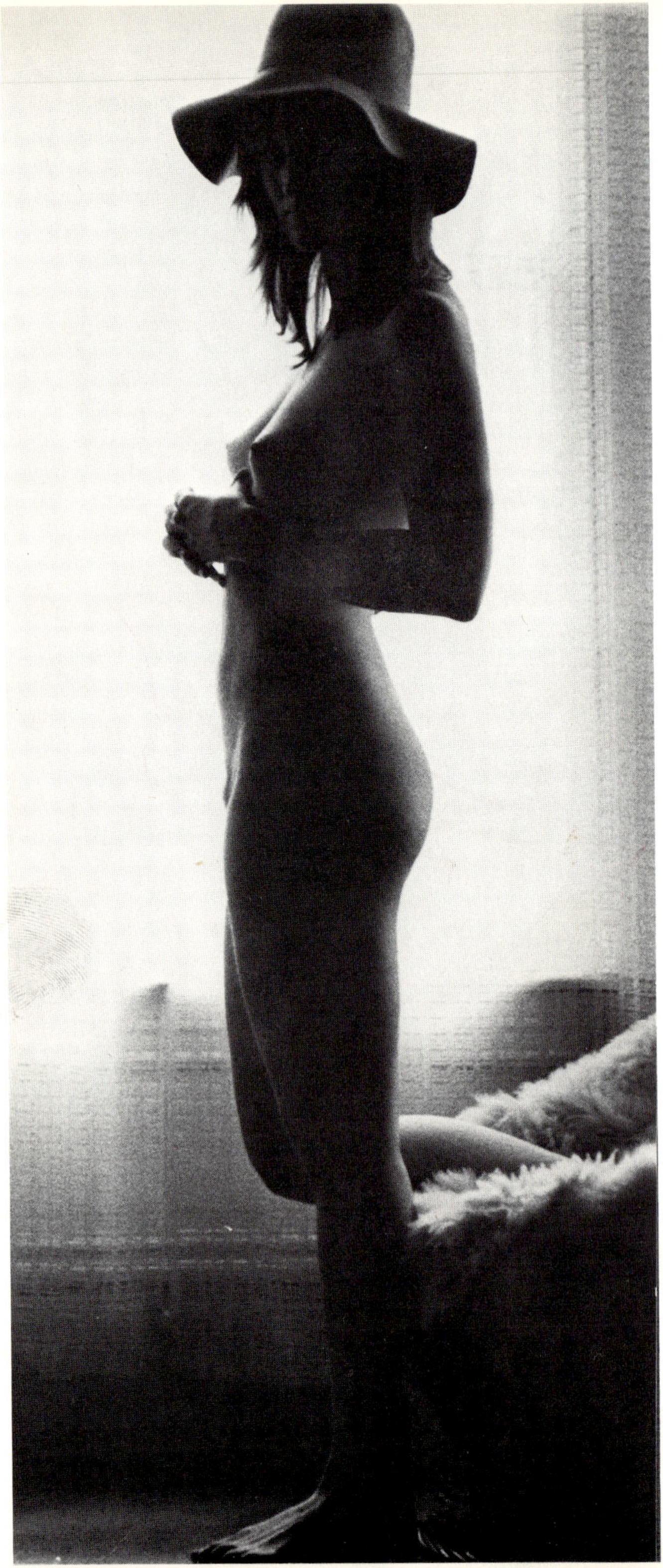

COLORS

I only cried
Three times in my life,
Once when I was born
Someone patted me on the ass
To see if I was alive.

Again, when I lost part of my mind
And it passed on, only to be blown
Away by dancing winds.

Once again, when overcoming my
Burning desire for smack and cocaine,
And then I started to love myself.

Now, when I feel your internal
Strokes, I could cry for a week,
Not from aimful pain,
But from a certain formula that always
Appears when you are present.

Yes, sometimes I be blacker than black
With a hidden vision calling softly
In the face of time, and I make my country
Aware of my suffering by battering down
Black, inky gravestones.

I found no shells in you,
No past plastic entrances.
I tanned your whiteness
That never got too white because you are
Without colors.

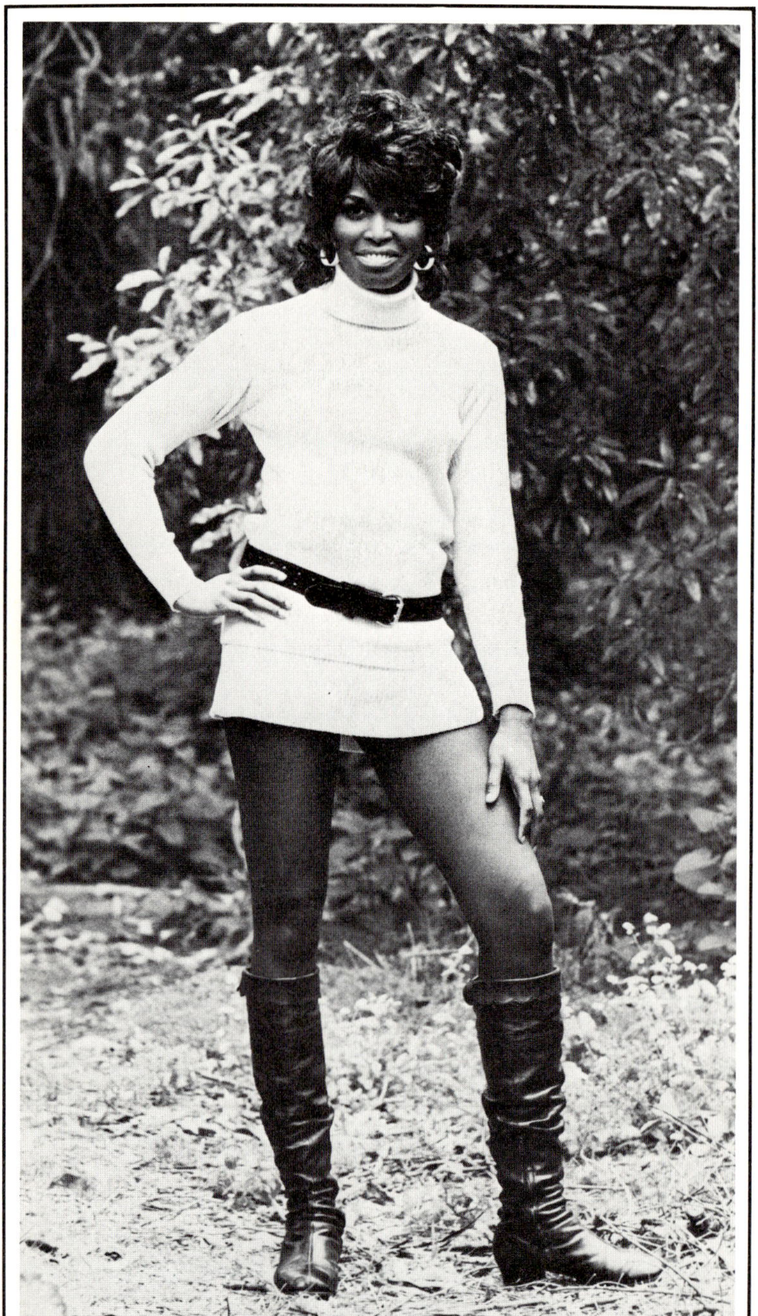

GIFTED
for Cecelia

Yes, sister
You're fine.
Sometimes in boots
And natural.

Your dark eyes shine
Like a flashlight,
The reflection sings back
Like a wordless song
From a silver flute.

From the shadows
Your walk becomes
A dance,
Dancing messages of being
Quiet and black.

If you missed the point,
Look at your insides,
It's mellowing
With being gifted.

NOWBYMYSELFNESS

Hey,
And I've been
Wondering

Why am I
So bymyself.
I went to get it,
But it wasn't there.
So here I am, looking
At it from here.

I plunge through time,
Searching for it.
I haven't got it yet,
But the search felt good.
Walking, confined to spirit and time.

Yes, blazing toward beauty,
Surrounded by hostile air, giving my
Unplanted self to one woman who opened
A Maverick Road through my nose.

We walked down New England Street.
Everything was right then, baby.
Unforgettable, positive shadows
As I learned.
Everything was right then, baby
As far as I saw it from there.

We didn't need miracles.
Whose sea mist, cool clouds
And flowers, magic fading dew.
At that time, from here, it was me
And you.

We were always going somewhere
With gentleness, lost in the Mediterranean,
And those skipping Sunday nights,
Moving the natural way, by nature.
But I never knew my unnaturalness
Was slowly ending.

Well,
And oh well,
Rhythm moved you
As the seashore moved.
Maybe it had to go down that way
From there, seeing it from here.

Rhythm beating, tearing pieces of
My mind.
You never said why. What hidden
Storm made your vine wind?
You smiled that friendship smile,
Like sunlight, but my soul still cried
For something more than friendship
When you passed.

In my bymyselfness, I'll cling
To some positive moment when
Rhythm and time move us back in existence.

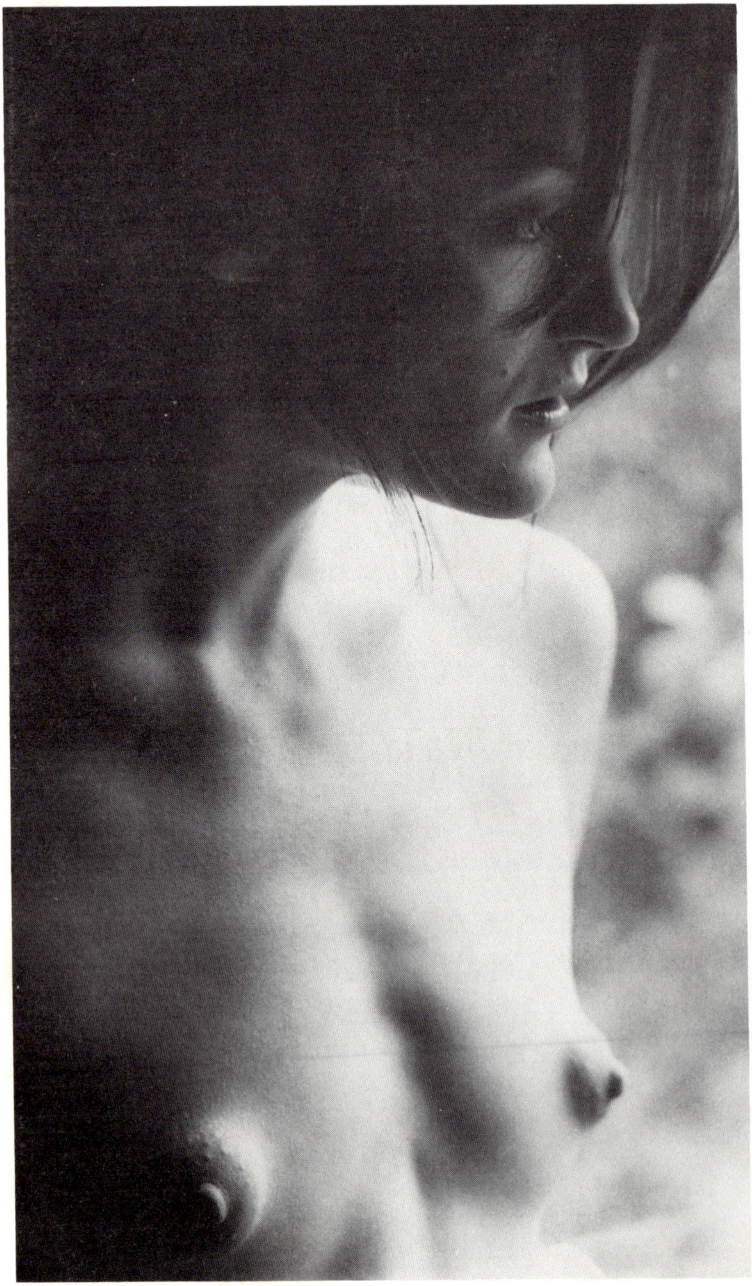

FLOATING IN FALLING TEARS

Picture me
In a quiet corner of your dreams
Six o'clock in the morning

And you got daylight blood
Made of sunshine
You forgot to turn the small radio off
With that terrible music

I knew it, hungry again
It's a common innocent loveliness
It's cool because it's spring

In your dream was I extending spirits
Into an orbit of magic?
Was I in your long Spanish hair?
Or floating in your falling tears

With your being a memory of
My India echoes
Was I memorizing the distance of space between us?

I remembered you in my music
You were the "GIRL OF THE YEAR"
That night
You excited the supreme

I found no sorrow about superimposing
Because you offered a texture to the
Center of my eyes

May your dreams be as real
As I have dreamed
And an instant memory of our possible range . . . .

I KNEW IT

Oh, yes,
I blew it.
I knew I blew it.
Total being, unaware
Of your mysterious paradise.

I blew it.
It's hammering in my brain.
Like summer rain.
I pushed eastward,
Carelessly following the voices
Telling me what to do.
With my mind so high,
Laid up with memories.

And there were fainted choruses,
Echoing and reforming rhythm,
Slipping against night shadows.
I plunged through time,
Time and seawinds, moaning.
Like a knife, the spirit of loneliness
Cut through my body.

I moved to the vibrations
Of a drum, the beating of your heart
Between the wise skies.
I saw a plastic dream
And heard an eternal song
Between tropical winds.

I knew it,
I knew it from moaning spirits.
I knew it from sunsets
And sundowns.
I knew it from C-C riders
And night coldness.
From time and hazel blue.
I blew it.
And that I knew.

I NEED YOU, AH, AHHHH

We traveled
With songs against
Your thighs
Playfully down between the warmth
And moist of your legs

And you started to cry portraits
Of my manhood
We had asserted a particularly beautiful day
Now we must unsophisticate a modern logic

First, come fly with me
And spirit my tongue
Let it rest between your pinkish lips
As I wait to feel your "I need you, ah, ahhhh
I need you, ah, ahhhh"
And the hesitating of your breath

Then the temptation of our being tempted
Made the distance shorter
We started to the Virgin Islands
To hear Latin rhythms and calypso laughter
But we seem to have been detained by the simplicity
Of being unsophisticated about our time
Thoughtfulness about our love of flesh
Sacred in melodies.

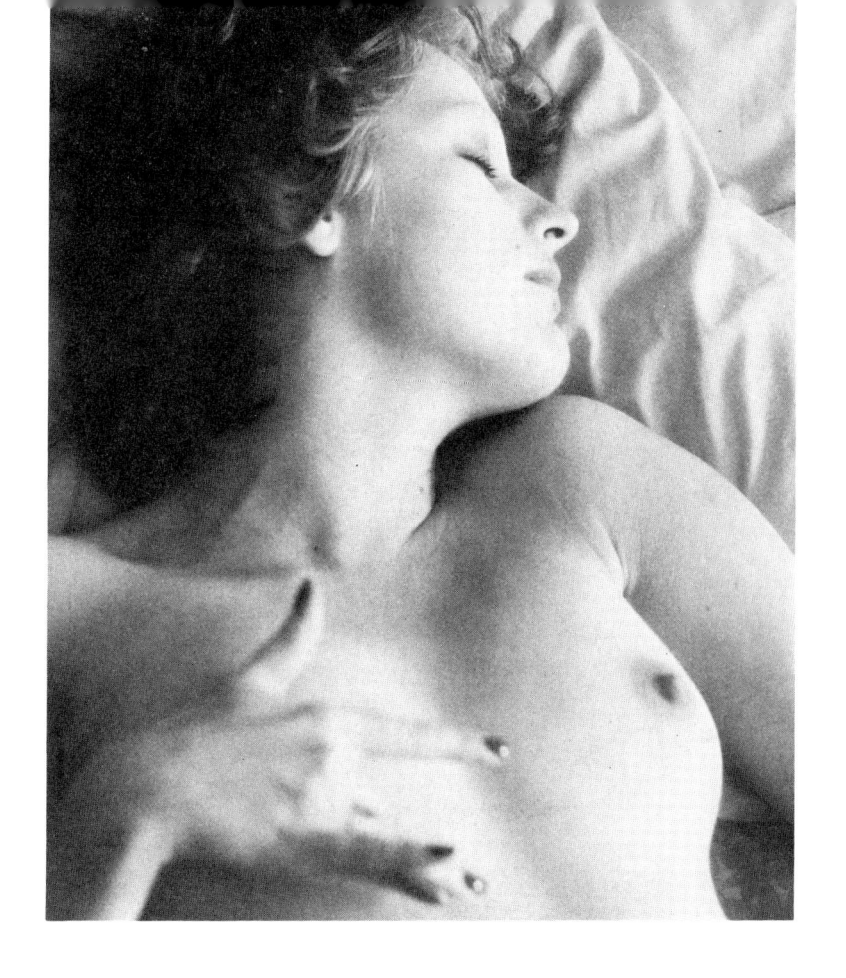

Now, oh!
Travel with me
Love with me
Sing with me
Dance with me
Pain with me
Be voices calling us away
Never leave without me
I need you, ah, ahhhh
I need you, ah, ahhhh . . . .

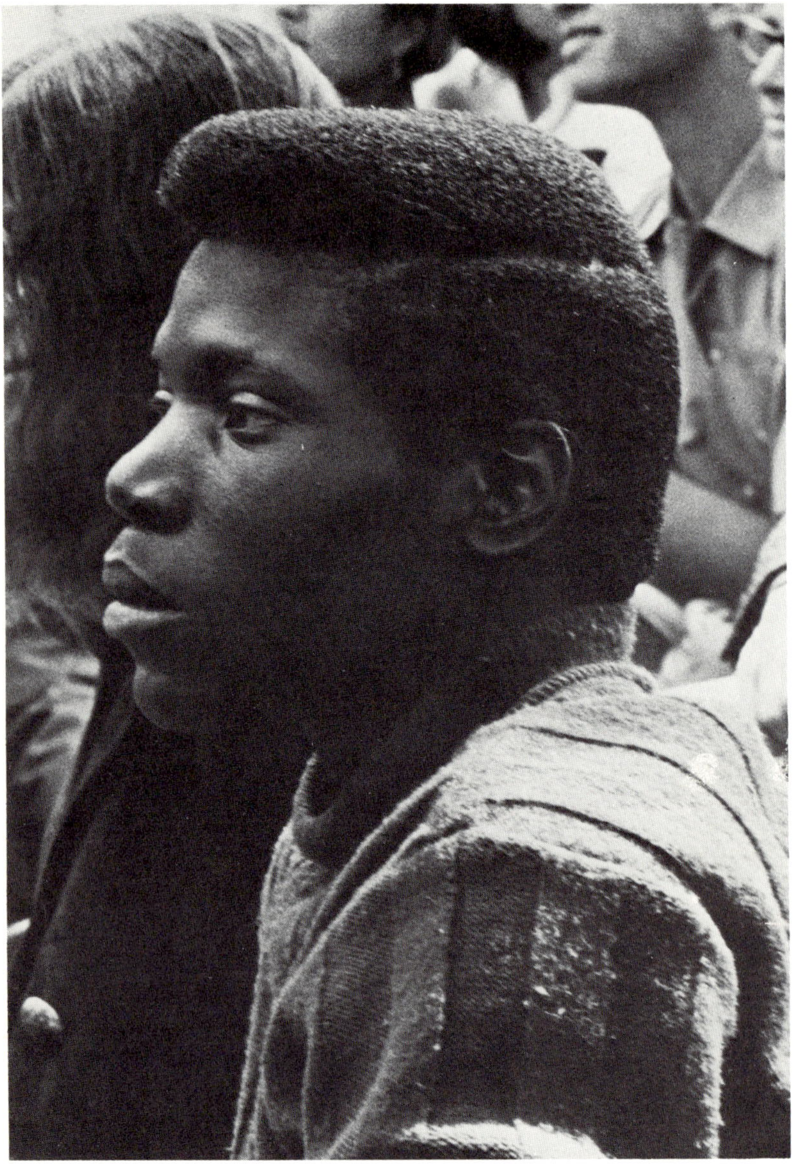

SOUL

Do you know what's wrong
With everybody today?
    There's always somebody
        Telling you what to be . . . and how to act
When all I'm doing is being
Black. Huh? Being black.

AND LOVE RULED THE WORLD

The angels started smiling
   This morning and lit up the world.
The angels flew over the troubled cities
   And made peace.

Angry Anglo-Saxons made peace
   With the Creator
Afro-Americans were pre-announced equal
   And all the presumptuous stigmas disappeared.

The angels flew through the church windows
   And united them, creating a universal spirit
So splendid that sinners laid down their deeds
   And pointed to the stars.

The angels spread their wings over white people
   And gave them a pigmented tan,
Put their white minds ashamed, making them
   Throw back their heads a thousand times,
Their racist voices choked and their tongues fell out.

I can hear the angels singing.
   Music was in the air.
Beethoven and Parker swung together.
   Nat Cole and Mahalia Jackson sung tales of beauty,
And the rainbow changed its colors.

And nobody lived underground, uptown or downtown.
    Subways, doorways and sidewalks all turned sideways,
The theme sounding all over the world,
    And love ruled the world.
Everybody learned understanding by singing
    "Come on, brother, let's do something together,
Let's pump some warm blood through our veins."

Black technicians for love, become outward.
    Be the inner breath. Breathe some love.
Drive out the space of man's nonvision.
    Pull some heads back. Block out the path of madness.
Fill the space with compassion.

Come on brother . . . come on.
    Don't you hear the angels?
Change up, brother. Touch your fingertips.
    Attach the portrait of God to the minutes
Of your finality. Open your eyes.
    The angels are black, like your ancestors
Through whom you came to this planet.
    You are attached to them like old cords.

Come on brother . . . come on.
    Imamu Amiri Baraka says, "It's nation time."
Nikki Giovanni says, "Black Judgment."
    The Last Poets say, "Black people, what y'all gon do?"
Gil Scott-Heron says, "The revolution will not be televised."
    Langston Hughes says, "The Negro speaks of rivers."

Without benefit of clarification, I say
    LOVE MUST RULE THE WORLD.

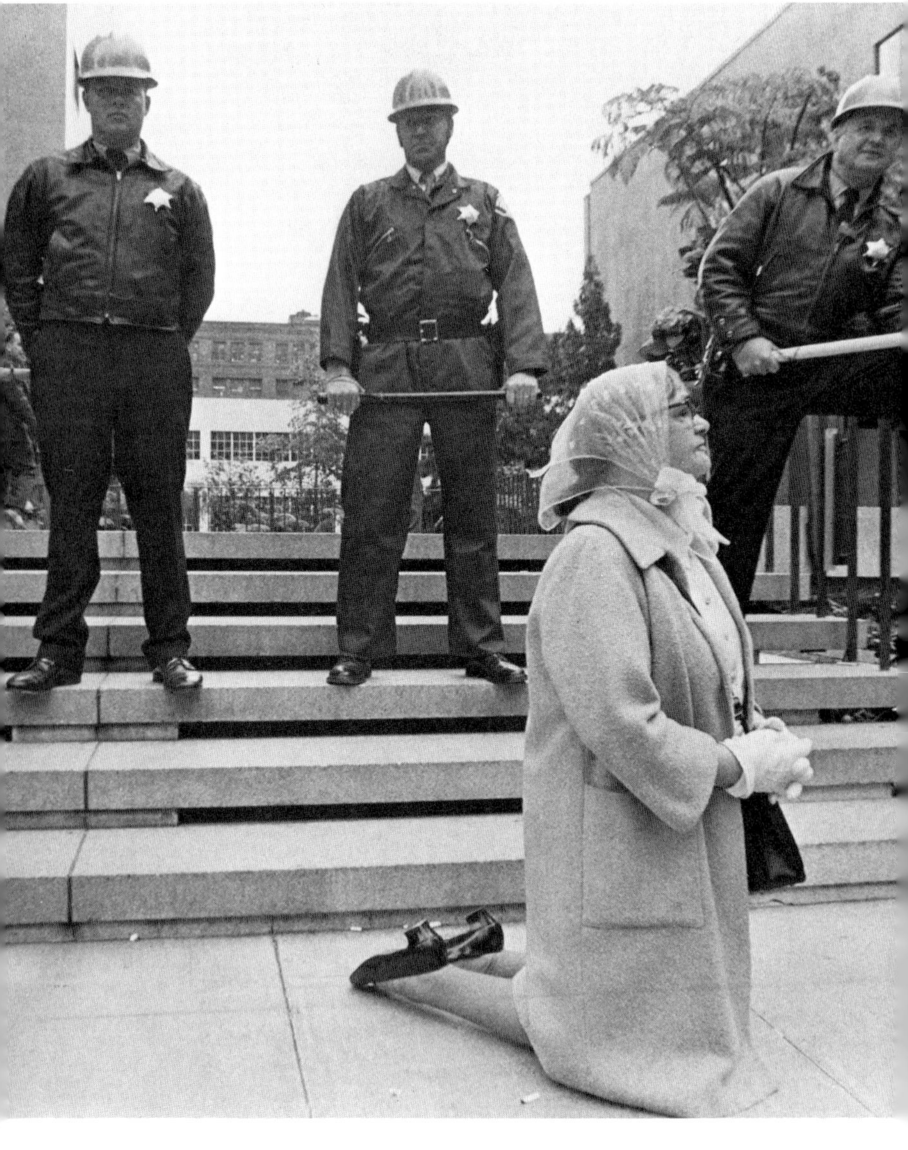

THE HUMAN PRAYER

GIVE me a symbol I can cling to
GIVE me a love I can retain
GIVE me an eye that can see inside of me
GIVE me a morning with no sorrow
GIVE me a word that I can say without offending anyone
GIVE me a heart that I can feel other's pressures
GIVE me a hand that I can reach out and touch a feeling
GIVE me a dream that I can make come true
GIVE me a spirit that I can commit myself to
GIVE me a testimony that I can make others understand
GIVE me the concept that I can understand my own mental revolution
GIVE me the strength for my own struggle for self-awareness
GIVE me the power of my subconscious mind
GIVE me the will to reinforce my values of a better life
GIVE me the understanding of my frustration when I'm pretending to be happy
GIVE me a song I can sing to let love ring
GIVE me a walk that will make me feel tall
GIVE me peace to influence my beliefs
GIVE me notes to myself to remind me of my weakness
GIVE me a creative mind to cope with my boredom
GIVE me a remote control of my thoughts so I may appropriate my decisions
GIVE me a respite for my image
GIVE me the configuration of most situations
GIVE me the wisdom to know the difference between love and hate
GIVE ME MYSELF

***IT'S A FACT THAT
NONE OF US
ARE REALLY
THAT BLACK***

You know, it's a fact
That none of us
Are really that black.

If we walk through
A city park
That same dog will bark.
All of us want a pleasing thrill,
And to shift gears uphill.
Isn't it a fact
That none of us
Are really that black?

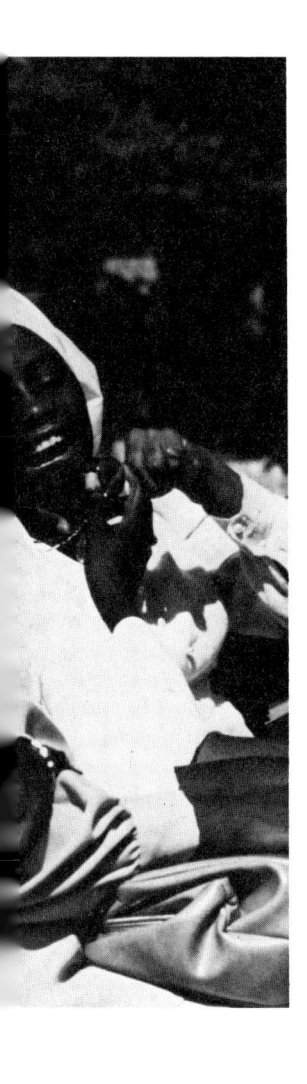

So what is there to life
That doesn't deal with living?
And what is there to taking
That doesn't deal with giving?
Most all of us believe in
Some kind of fate.
And in our solitary confinement,
We learn to cope with hate.
In every heart there is some pain.
And every race and color
Plays the same old game.
Do you know it's a fact
That none of us
Are really that black?

Beneath our cold bloody skin
No one may understand
Our conflictness.
But when the pinwheel enters
The center of our heart,
We all got the same sickness.
We search for a description
To translate our desire,
And try to select the right
Mate to smother our fire.
Don't you see it's a fact
That none of us are
Really that black?

I wonder somehow if I can
Make you understand.
Now, just turn over your hand
If you can,
And think of the weakness
Of every man.
It's all created by a
Master plan
That no one really owns this land.
Stolen, leased, borrowed, bought
It remains a universe
Where nations have fought.
Let our Mexican brother,
Who also has to fight,
Stand up for his right.
And our Indian brother
This country was stolen from,
Can't go into town at night.
Our Asian brother, we can't
Always pronounce his name,
So we say he's strange.
Can't you see it's a fact
That none of us
Are really that black?

I might pass a white man
Shopping in a store.
In his mind, he might think,
"I won't come here anymore."
But somewhere in the hills
Or on the street, we'll meet
Some place.
And we'll have the same unfriendly
Looks on our faces.
Meanwhile, across town,
A black brother is down,
And doesn't agree,
Because he's trying
To be blacker than me.
Let's pretend that we're all gold
But don't feel the same - -
But we got the same blood in our vein.
Tell me, doesn't anybody know
What color is pain?
So, isn't it a fact
That none of us
Are really that black?

IF I COULD PERSUADE THE WORLD

If I could persuade the world
The magic word would be FREE
I would let it be
And pain would have no name
If I could persuade the world.

If I could persuade the world
The wind would stand still
And the rivers would yield
And trees would stand tall
As the rainbow would fall
There would be no outstanding
Dues to pay
And there would be peace
Night and day.

If I could persuade the world
The world would stand still
And every man would
Forget how to kill
There would be love from the start
And we all would have an equal part
Dreams would be made real
Music would become our theme
Tranquility would be the scene
With halves made whole
And only truth would be told
If I could persuade the world.

If I could persuade the world
I would open the eyes of the blind
Bring brotherhood to the divine
Worship in a sacred place
Let there be the same
Color on our face
If I could persuade the world.

If I could persuade the world
I would let the whole world sing
And no one would experience pain
The entire world would change
If I could persuade the world.

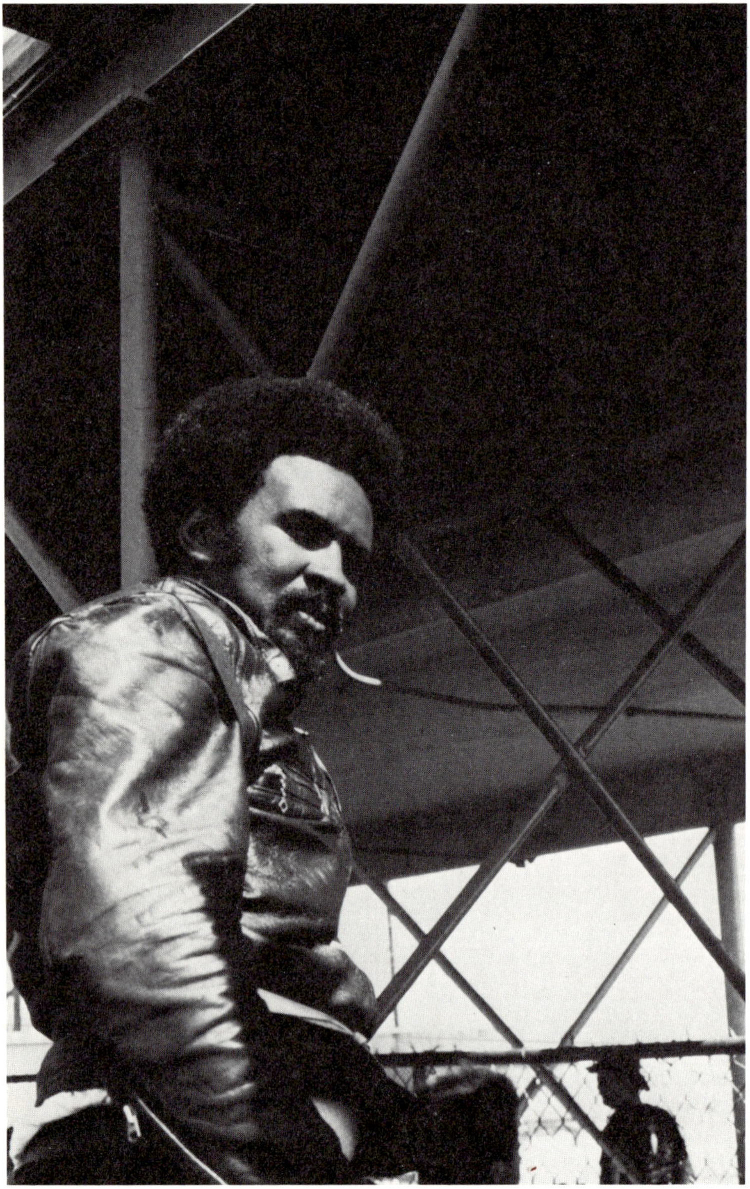

SAGITTARIUS

       evil
       live
Egotism expressing designs to be
    ugly beyond hate, extreme self-denial.

Violation of existence, falsehood, never natural,
    shaped by unassumed movements between recess.

Instant, spontaneous retribution, retrieved by heart.

Leaving beliefs for pain, awaiting blind
    logical structures intensified
    by price not worth paying.

Language, poetry, rhythmic sex
    exhibit of masculinity.

Innerworld directed by energy, extension,
    supersubstitutions and loving by external
control.

Vibrations in Sanctuary, birth, Sagittarius, Jupiter
    influence making happiness.

Essence, earth, music
    everything is life before death.

ON BLACK

Black
    On black
Black when trying not
    To be black
Black, dirty black
    Half black.

Black even when forgot
    To be black
Black never letting me
    Forget I'm black
Black when white becomes black.

    Sad black,
    Jazz black,
    Funeral black, wearing black.

Black evil
Black existence
Black blues, be cool black
    Night black
Black cat
    Bad-luck black
    Little black book
    Bad cowboy, black hat.

Black day
Black eye
    Turns black
    White shows up better on black
Black stove, cook black
    Burns black
    No good, placed in the garbage can black
Black smoke, destroyed black.

White on blackwall tires
White shirt
    Clean white
    Wash white
    Good white folks
    Keep clean white
    Snow White, Cinderella white
    Sleeping Beauty white
    Elizabeth Taylor, five-time loser, white
    Little Jack Horner white
    Angel white
    Admired, atmosphere white.

White veil, purity white
    Wedding in white
White hospital, white liner
White doctor in white
White shows up black
White background
White minds white
    Got you believing white
    Sucking white air white
Invisible
    Red blood
Ain't black on white a brown bitch!

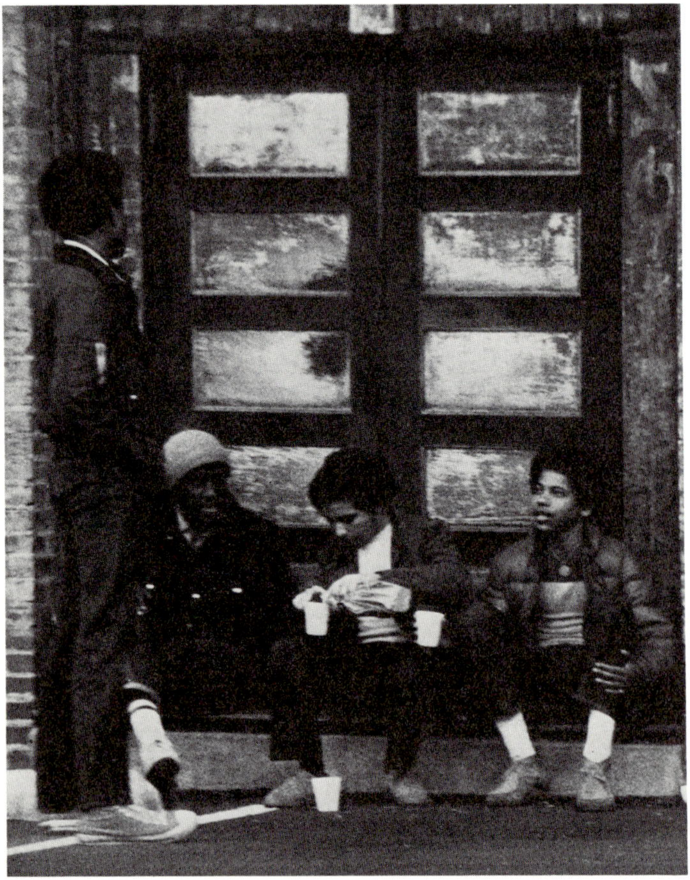

HONORARY

I got my honorary degree
From the ghetto,
No colleges,
Just inferior schools
And poverty programs that didn't work.

The ghetto is a concentration camp.
I saw brothers and sisters blood baptizing
In the street
At least twice a week.
Boogalooin, goodfootin and deteriorating
From oppression.

Now, I moved from the ghetto,
So my brothers called me a traitor,
Because I didn't wait for the black massacre
And re-enslavement.

But I heard the word of God
He also slept in a hollow log
And was mistreated like a dirty dog.
My spiritual logic IS . . .
God helps those who
Get up and move . . . .

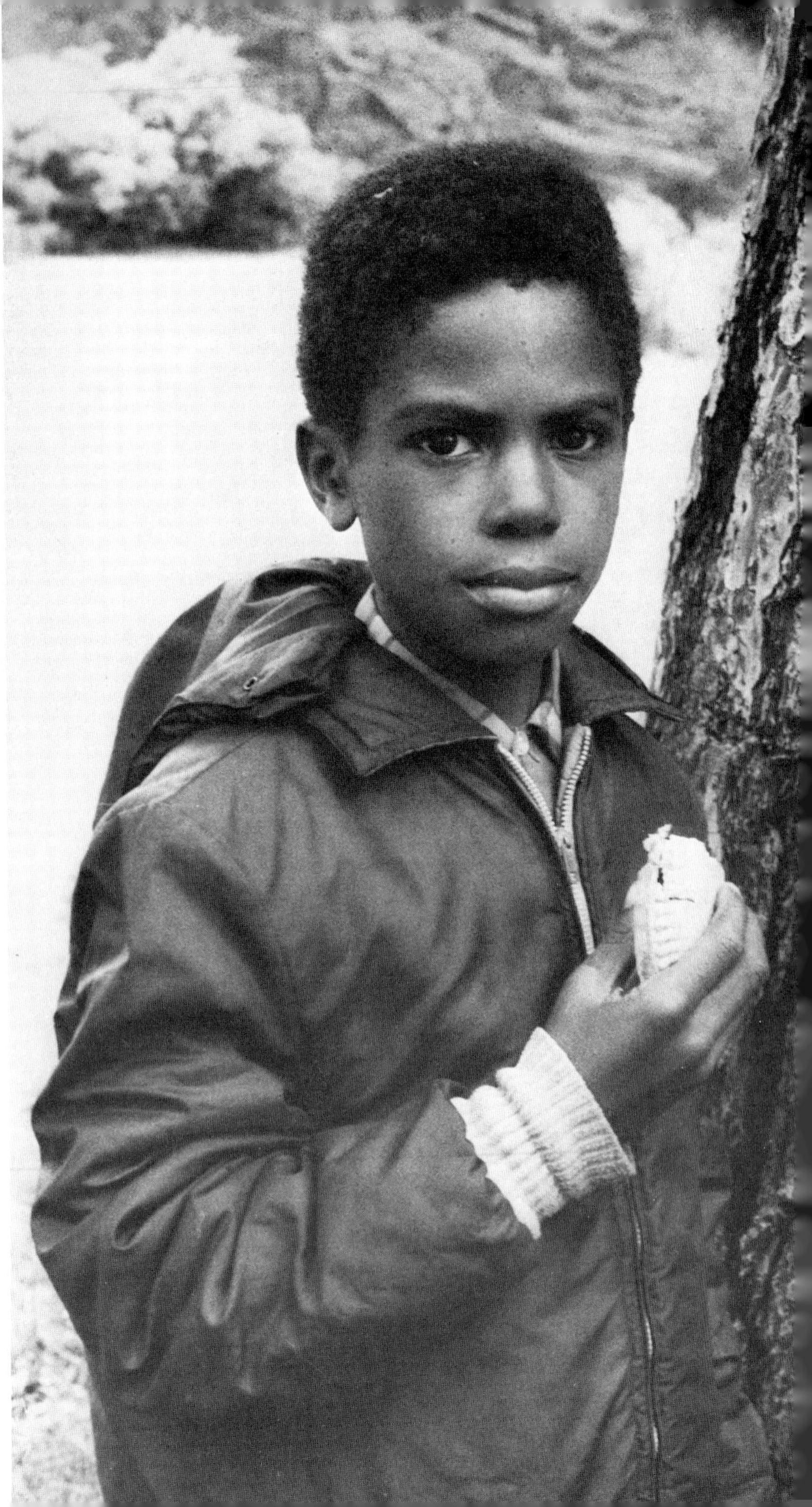

DON'T BURN MY BLACK OFF

I was born under the sun,
And the moon moved over.
And I came up being a subject,
That's why I'm so dark.
It was the moon, wasn't it?

God related my darkness,
As he chose not to transform
Me into the sheep that cry of
Frustration. But may my cries
Be of liberation.

Being what I am, what I'm continuing
To be, brilliant, talented, capable of
Freedom. Free of the white-minded hatred.
I'm adding dimensions that the naked
Eye can't see.

The power of equation may be at work.
Tell me the great wilderness is free,
Or the fire will not burn the black
Off my face, but burn love in my heart.

Too clearly, the social storm
Moves in the opposite direction,
While my knowledge of it travels.
Too many stolen hearts from Africa
Make me seek explanations
For my denial.

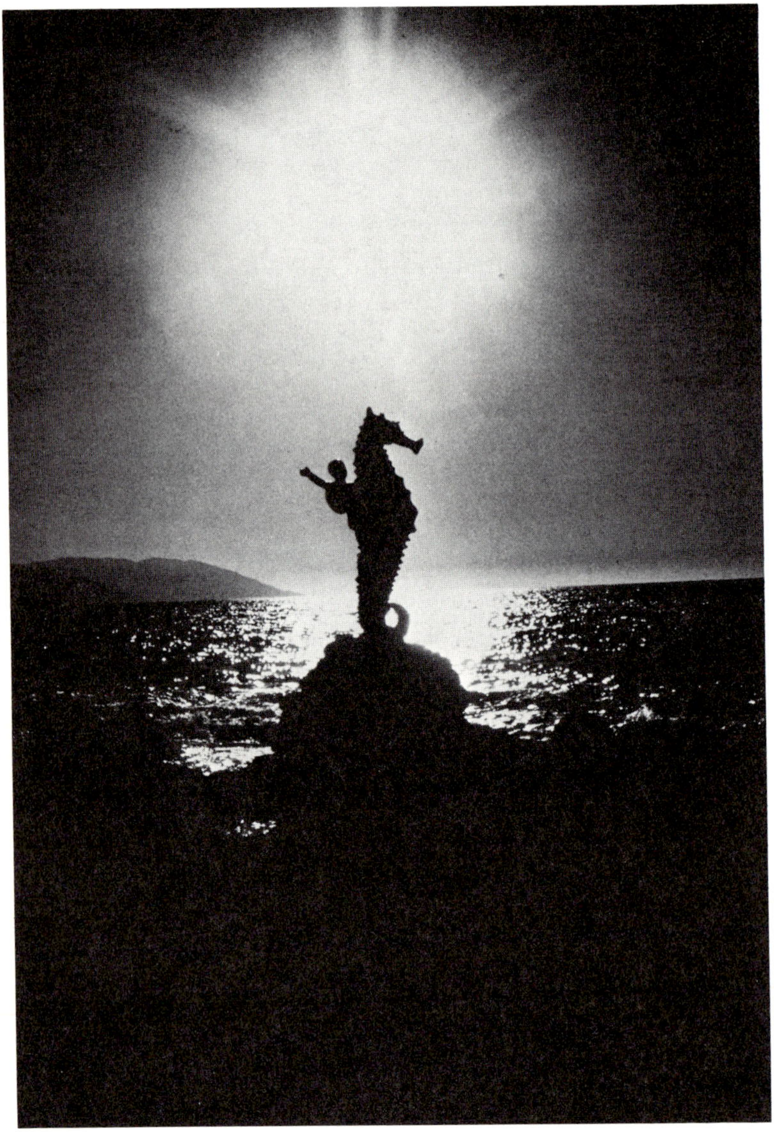

THE WAR LORDS

They came on ships,
They came wearing white hats,
They came on horses,
They came with whips and chains,
They changed our forefathers' names.

They came like vampires,
Sucking like Dracula's bite.
They came with fire at high noon
And no morals at night.
They came wearing masks and hoods
To keep their faces out of sight.

They gave brass spoons
And plastic cups, but they used silver.
They kept a watchful eye as the plants grew,
But they forgot the planted seeds of Africa
Would grow into a mighty people,
Sprouting limbs of insurrection.

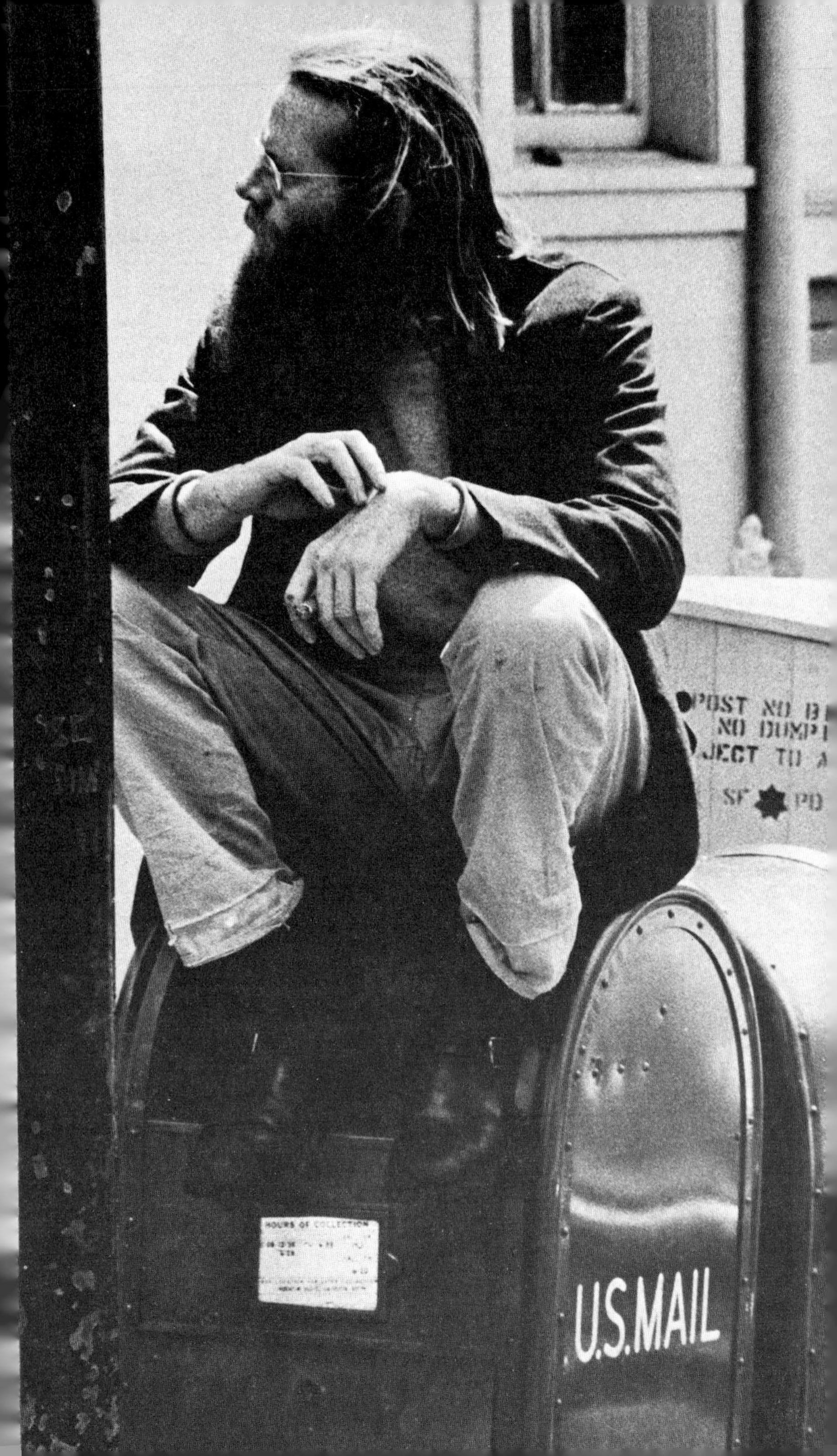
HOURS OF COLLECTION
U.S.MAIL

ASTRONAUTS

Up, up, go up!
    With them who send
        Wicked astronauts for moon walks.
They may find history significant,
    As they come home like a dog
        With a bone.
Crowing a monkey-jungle-brain
With lame, righteous, insane,
Prefabricating moon dust.

We're down here
    Digging on the plot
        I cannot complete my love—
Making without checking on birth
    Control. My balls and valuables
        Went to Cape Kennedy to prepare
For a moon shot. The shot was so hard
It ruptured my spleen.

The earth is always counting faces.
    Redman counts anything.
    Yellowman takes advice.
    Badman goes sour.
    Whiteman counts power.
Liberators tortured by jet prisons.
Love so rare, anywhere,
Even up there.

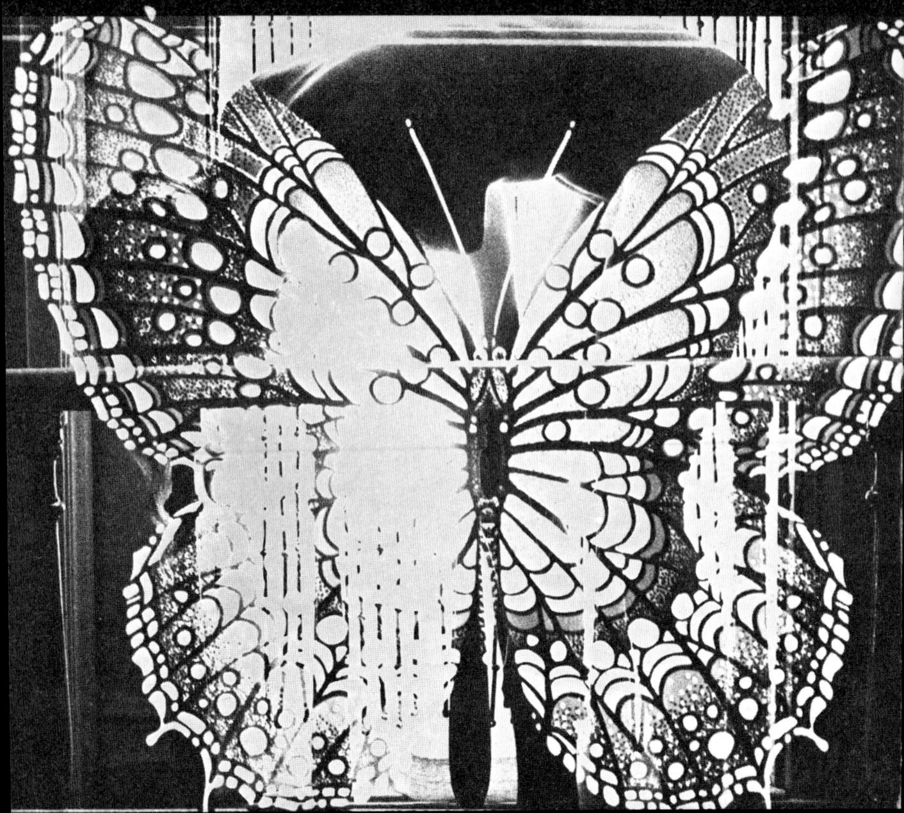

ON A FUNKY TRIP

Are you looking for me? Look on.
    You won't find me.
    Because I'm dancing,
    Dancing to the thunder of indescribable
    Rhythm.
Genius, rise in spirit. Rise, genius.
    I'll be a positive energy in space.
    From rubber snakeheads to the
    Black Lagoon.

If you don't see me, I'm dancing
    Behind a hoop of
    Bleeding eyes
    For human form.
Dancing with a decade of wax bitches
    Trapped in their own complexions.

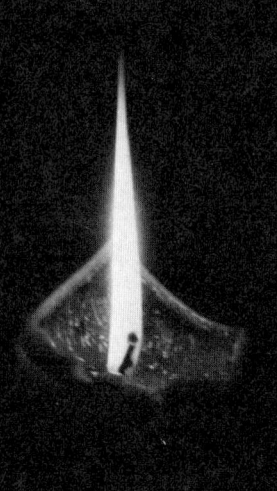

If you're searching for me,
 I'm on a psychedelic way-outness.
 I'm a positive demagogue.
 I'm the actual take-over of myself.
Just before everything, to do anything.
  Dancing to the imaginary
  Shape of one million degrees
  Over a foggy yesterday.

If you can't find me,
    I'll be writing poems.
      Poems about the funky universe
      And its historical moans,
      Unknown to human spirits.
I'll write about elephant asses
      Sitting on ant tails
      And kissing fleas
      While watching airplanes take off
      From this old nation.

If you send for me, send for a
    Complete subject in space.
      My face will be covered
      With maps of this dead nation,
      A nation too dead to rise.

I'll write about emptiness,
    Witches and devils,
    Animals who call themselves humans.
    I'll write about the west,
    North, east, and south.
I'll write about a history that
    Taught some to hate.
    I'll be dancing to freedom,
    Freedom that I've never known.
    I'll write about blackness.

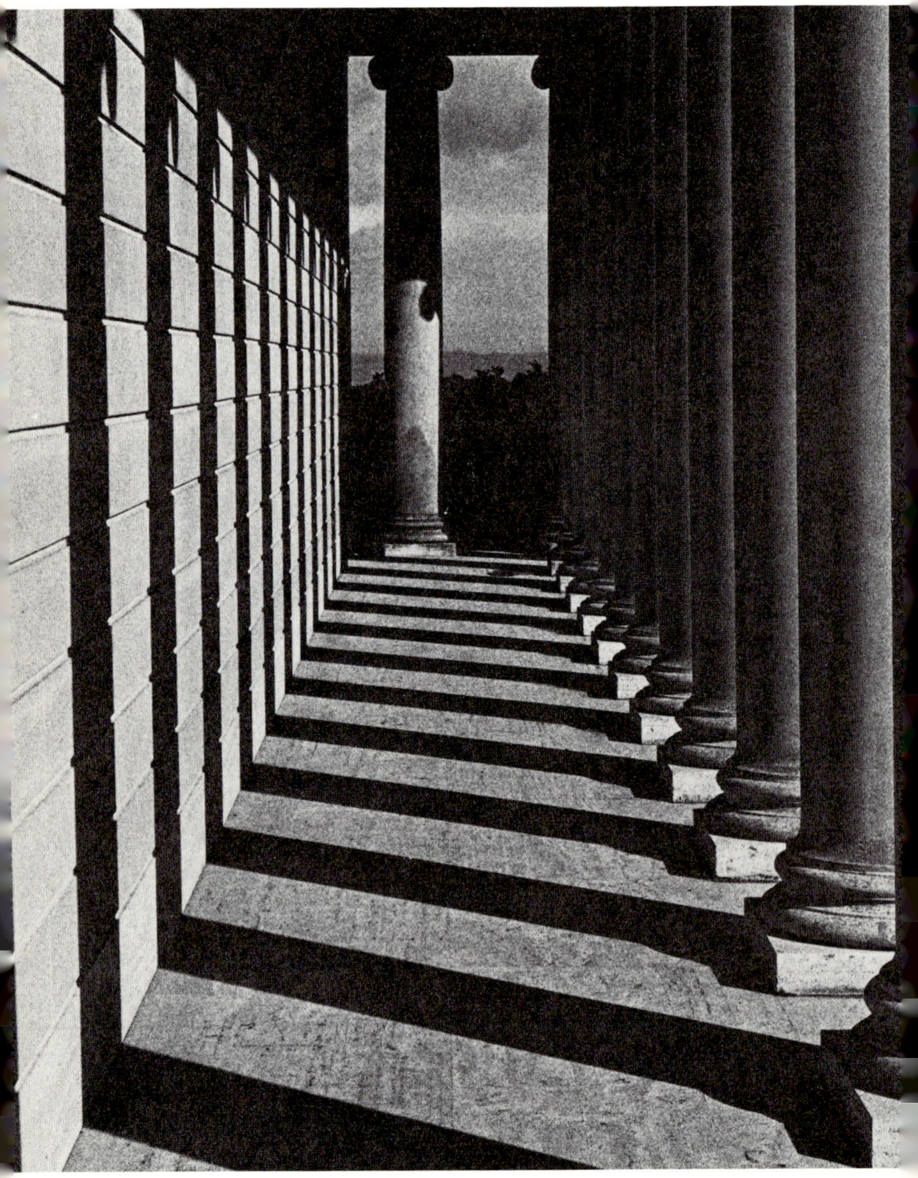

FEELING GUILTY

When I feel guilty
And have no defense
I wait for justice
Knowing I should use
Common sense.

Walked in and out of the
Courtroom feeling that I've
Been had, couldn't afford a good
Lawyer so I may lay up in jail
Feeling sick and mad.

I remember the judge's face
Sick, white and pale
As he asked me to step forward
He knew damn well I had failed.

I could've got a public defender
If I could've found one home
But I had heard that they're always
Writing things down wrong.
After all, 90 days ain't long
So I'll wait my time.
When asked "How did it go?"
I'll say fine.

IT'S TIME TO BECOME

It's time to become
    What you are
        becoming

Like chestnuts
On a tree
We fall
We keep falling down
From overripeness
        and trembling cold

We crack,
We roll like chestnuts
        until we're picked up

We watch empty space disappear
To whereabouts unknown
Sometimes reappearing by tenth cousins
        trying to become
        a postitive magnetism
        in slow motion

We're placed in bags
Sometimes with other nuts
        who roll around
        until together we crack
        or
        change up

It's time to become
Natural time
Inner self on notice to naturalness
        of self

It's time out for being unclean pollution
Running wild in yesterday's direction
It's real special to become
        reborn before death takes your time

It's time to be nappy-headed and black
without shouting
shhhh, shhhh

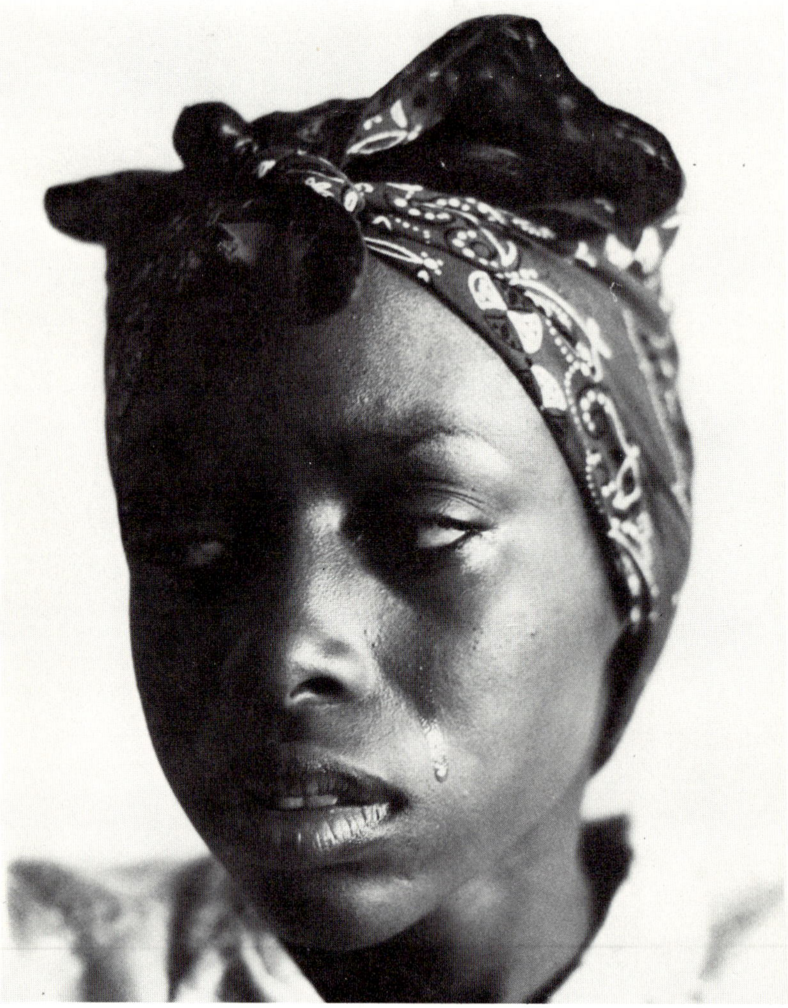

SLAVERY AS MY SUBJECT

Stand beneath time, because there is time.
Time to do it. Time related to a thousand
Reformed faces. Golden autumn and warrior ships.
Thrusts of boundless souls as the supreme God watched.

Heaven must not forsake the fury of
Black bones. On the wit of greatness,
I declare slavery as my subject.
My tongue clings to the roof of my mouth.
I'll find words to proclaim my manhood
That you stripped from me.

I once hesitated to show you my soul,
But now I will no longer be my advisor
Because I have become literate,
As literate as Frederick Douglass,
Richard Wright, and W.E.B. DuBois.

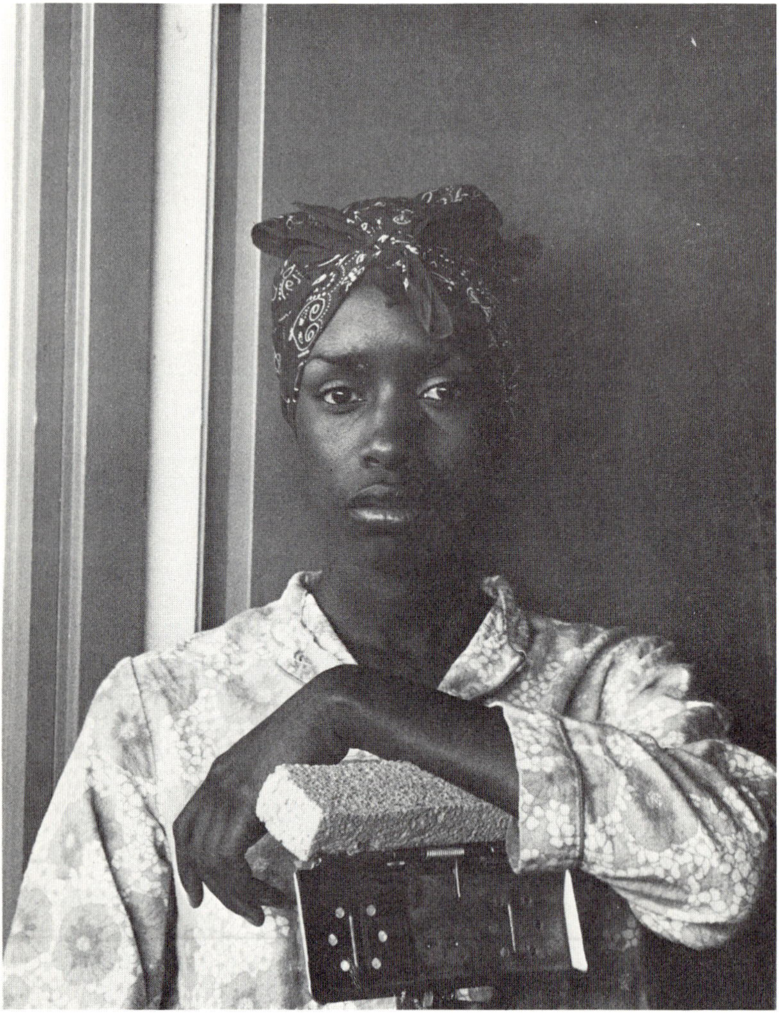

While you burned and suppressed
Many brutal words, my heart became
Shattered, but persistent.
My spirit stronger.
No adhesive can cover the wounds.

My flesh no longer mourns
From slavery's poison, that sickened my
Soul at night when I dreamed of freedom.

My father bled.
I may not have blood to give.
So I will give my flesh to demand freedom.
I cannot bleed; neither will I be driven to
Hostile existence.

May the supreme creator
Speed the time when human blood
Will not be in the path of our fathers,
But in the nature of human rights.
Then we can bury Civil Rights
With the bones of the old, colored
Supernigger, as he died singing, "WE SHALL OVERCOME."

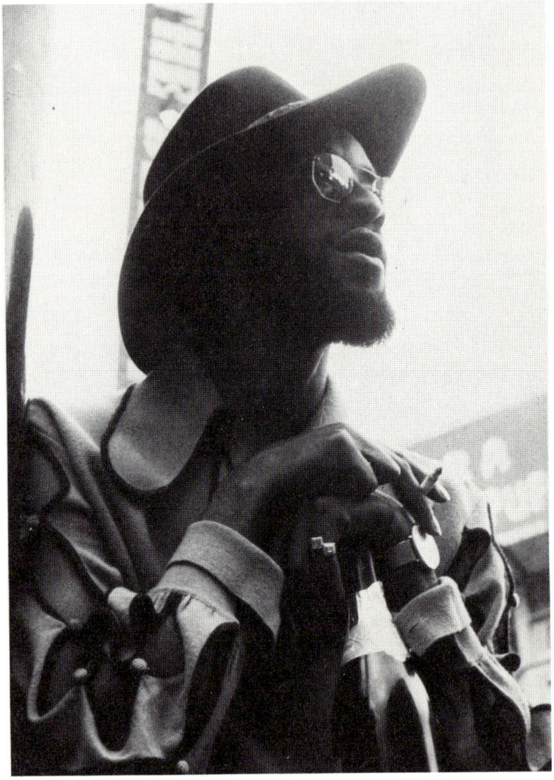

I'M JUST BEING BLACK

Do you know what's wrong
With everybody today?
    There's always somebody
       Telling you what to be . . . and how to act
When all I'm doing is being
Black. Huh? Being black.

Got my jams and my tape on loud.
Yeah! Blowing cool.
    Zipping past,
    Finger poppin'
    With my superbadass.

Sharp! Looka here.
Sporting a pinstripe suit,
    Double-breasted coat.
    Now, me? I don't need smack.
I'm so culturally turned on. Just listening to
The Temptations and being black.

I walk with a Kansas City dip,
Falling in love,
    Being cool, and talking hip.
    I don't see ghosts.
Love to roll them sheets,
Make the chicks cry.
    I don't smoke weed;
    I'm just culturally high.
Listening to sounds, using tact.
Huh! Jawjiving . . . being black.

Now, you see, white folks don't understand
The secret talks and walks
    Of the black man.
    When we say, "Right on! It's yo thang."
    (Not, "It's your thing.")
And like, "Mellow groove, I've got the bitch's mind."
"Copping dates" and "signifying."
    That's an image, not a fact.
    It's part of my culture, baby.
    Feeling good . . . being black.

Now, words like dictation, manifestation,
Organization, accumulation,
    Stockmarket robbers,
    And razor cut barbers,
Those 'er white words, we don't use those
"A little dab'll do you—Brylcream,"
    When I use
    Afro—Sheen.
    Shhhh . . . .

Now, I'm not prejudiced.
I look over my shoulder at white girls,
    Black ones, too.
    I'm no freak.
    When the lights are out,
    Either one will do.
I was born with that knack,
Plenty soul, gettin' it on,
    Being black.

I strode into the White House the other day.
You know, walkin' this way.
    I could hear Nixon say,
    "Why did that boy turn his back?"
    I said, "I don't dig your speeches,
    So I'm just being myself,
    Being black."

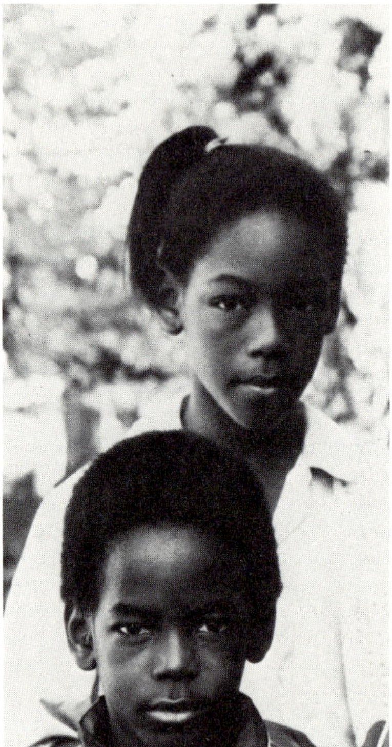

POEM FOR MY SISTER
for Sylvia

I recall the little girl
With the strong legs,
The loving arms that held so tightly,
And the hands that wouldn't let go of my shirt.
She dragged me through the many bushes
And hills, as the hot sand made me
Want to turn back for another start tomorrow.
The tension sometimes seemed terminal.

Getting out of breath,
My face turning pale on occasions
As a loving gray-headed old lady
Shouted, "Praise the Lord!"
The little girl seemed relieved that the
Old lady was pleased with the return of
The angels.

"You shall drink water from the
Blessed cup. It will make you strong.
You will live in the image of Heaven,"
As I am softly tucked into bed.
Then the steam from the pot on the stove
Starts to clear my breathing passages
And I fall off to sleep.

Early morning, I'm awakened by
The little girl with the strong legs.
"When the stove gets hot, you can
Get ready for school," she said
As she selects my warm clothes.

Off to school. "You all don't walk
Too fast now"
As the wise old lady with the serious glance
Closed the door and knelt to pray.
Her selective words rang in the air
Like the words of a prophet.

I stumbled throught the hills
As the little girl who buttoned my coat
Directed our journey.
There will be many stops, and a prayer
For it not to rain.
Then the sun shines from above the pine trees,
And the little girl smiles,
For she knows the journey will be a safe one.

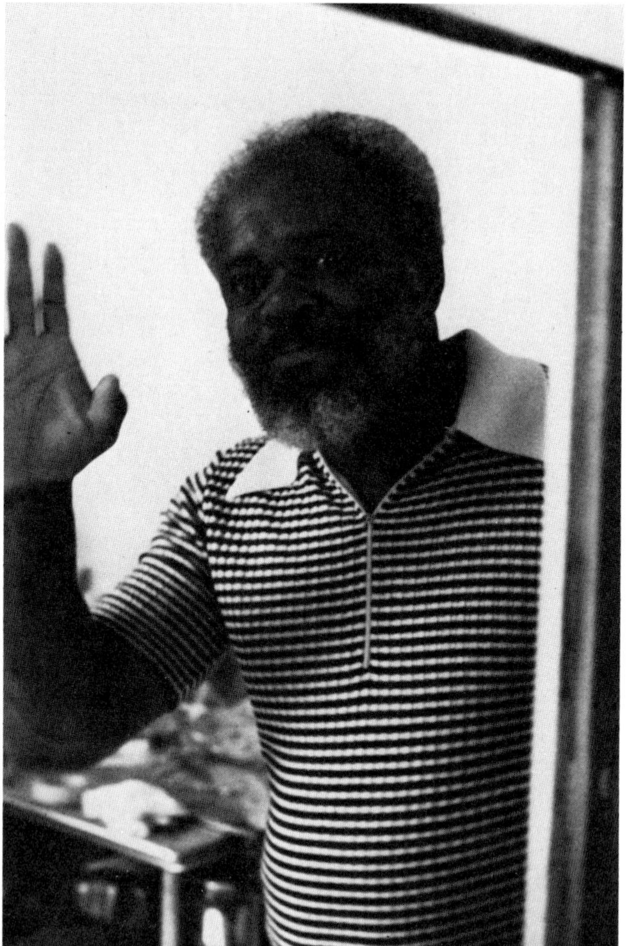

CONSCIOUS

Little comes to those who wait
                To loom, boom, pulling too soon.
Out of a gesture's thrust,
                You missed the combination
When your mind drifted away.

                I tried to explain it.
Three o'clock in the morning,
                Up in Detroit
When I had enough of those Goddamn
                Civil Rights, and I'm still
No more satisfied.

You see, I'm considered an upstanding
                Gentleman, with superfine principles
Written on the head of my penis.
                And where I put it categorizes me.
And in a poem I wrote, you called me names
                Because I didn't uplift mournful
Grievers by saying Honkie and Cracker more often.

You see, I converted words to heart
                And if it gets too painful, I'll shoot
Some love to it instead of heroin.
                Great fools in school may lose
Their minds, so somebody better be conscious.

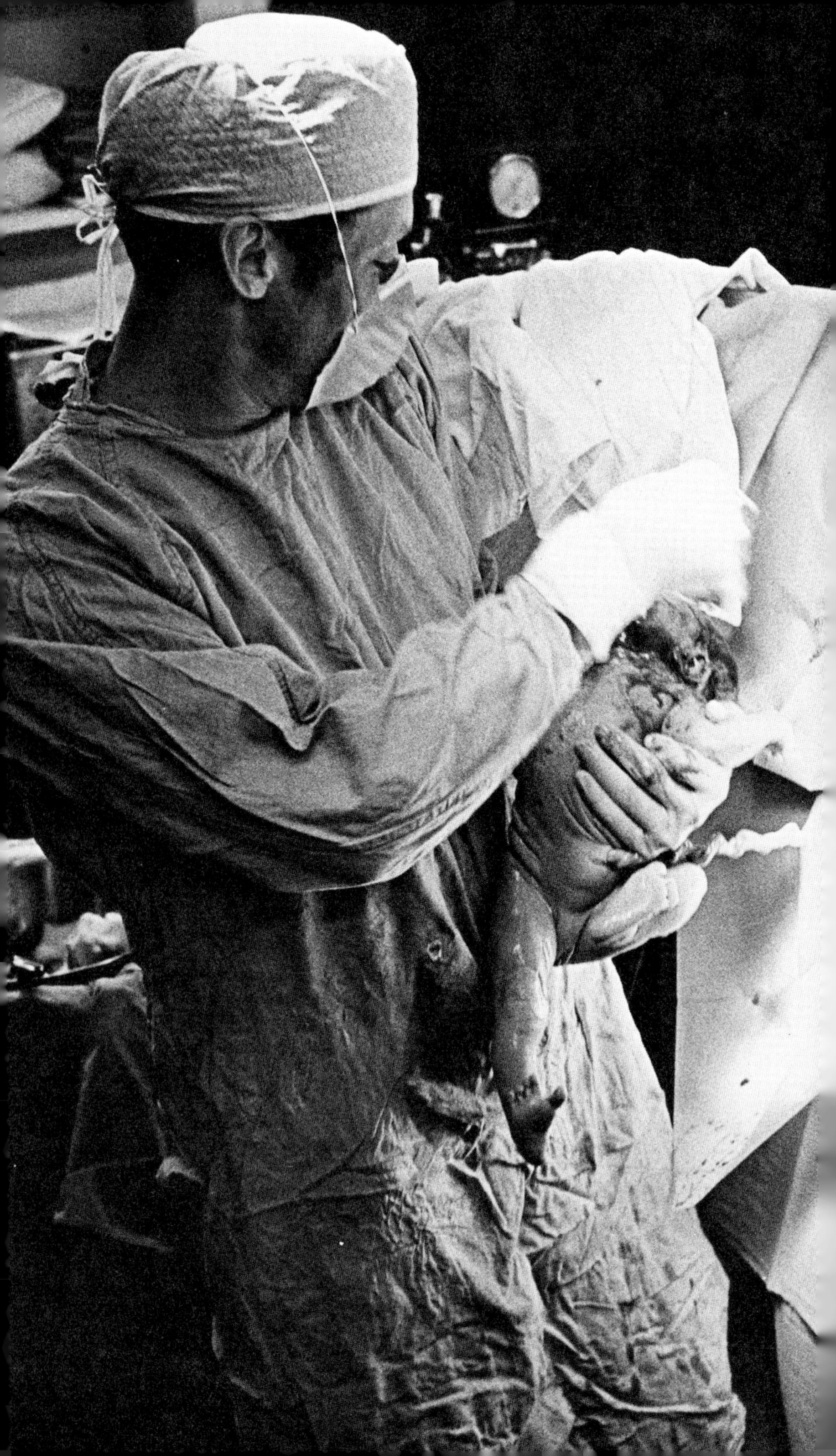

INTROSPECTION

From the womb I came
While some memories remain.
It's so easy to overlook the dazzling light
And hope for the answers that are right.
My skin, a memory strange as the water through a dam.
Back home to blackness,
I don't know who I am.

I may be a gift to me
I should know, so all soul-less attempts
Can never possess me if I am identified with wrong.
I must confess my exit as a drummer
Beating a flam. Sometimes
I don't know who I am.

I sit down with myself
While many black warriors are dying
I keep many secrets about myself
Some know I am lying. I frequently forget
I am the most critical person of me I've seen
If it appears I don't give a damn, it's not true.
It's because
I don't know who I am.

CELL BLOCK NO. 5

I'd rather not go
If you can find
Someone else.

I'm afraid
Of being caught
With rubber thumbs.

And another summer
Being locked in solitude.
Freeze the time, for I
Have not grown my beard yet.

Stop the clock.
I'm alive. No man ever
Left here without seeing a
Million pale faces blackened with fear.

Let the ground have it's caves
And the screws have their cells.
I never called a cop a "pig"
Until I came here.

I may never smell
Shalimar perfume again
Or forget the luxurious moon
Moving with the patient winds.

Perhaps it will rain.
I may never know the orange skies,
Sunshine, and magic words.

I may see my life
Floating in the clouds
I dreamed about.

April may form spring,
Uttering such golden texture.
And modern jazz played outside
Cell Block No. 5
And contemporary generations
Digging on a new future without me.

My cell is locked.
Echoes of keys are not the
Proper sounds. Please bring
Low voices of the winds,
If you can find someone else
I'd rather not go.

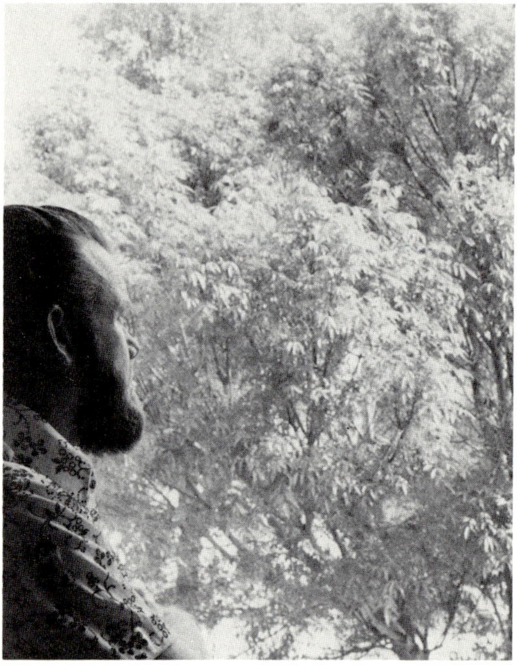

THE MAN WHO DOESN'T HAVE TO BE BLACK
for Don Wilson

A man who had nothing but something
To give, if you can get it
Because you got to get it
If you can dig it.

His words go beyond
Grace and glory
Sounding against your image
Telling the story.

If you happen to be a black man
All words must be rebuffed
To travel over your horizon.

One night I closed my eyes
And forgot to see his color
I forgot to sharpen my weapon
And he ambushed me.
Now I have grown
Accustomed to a friend
Who doesn't have to be black.

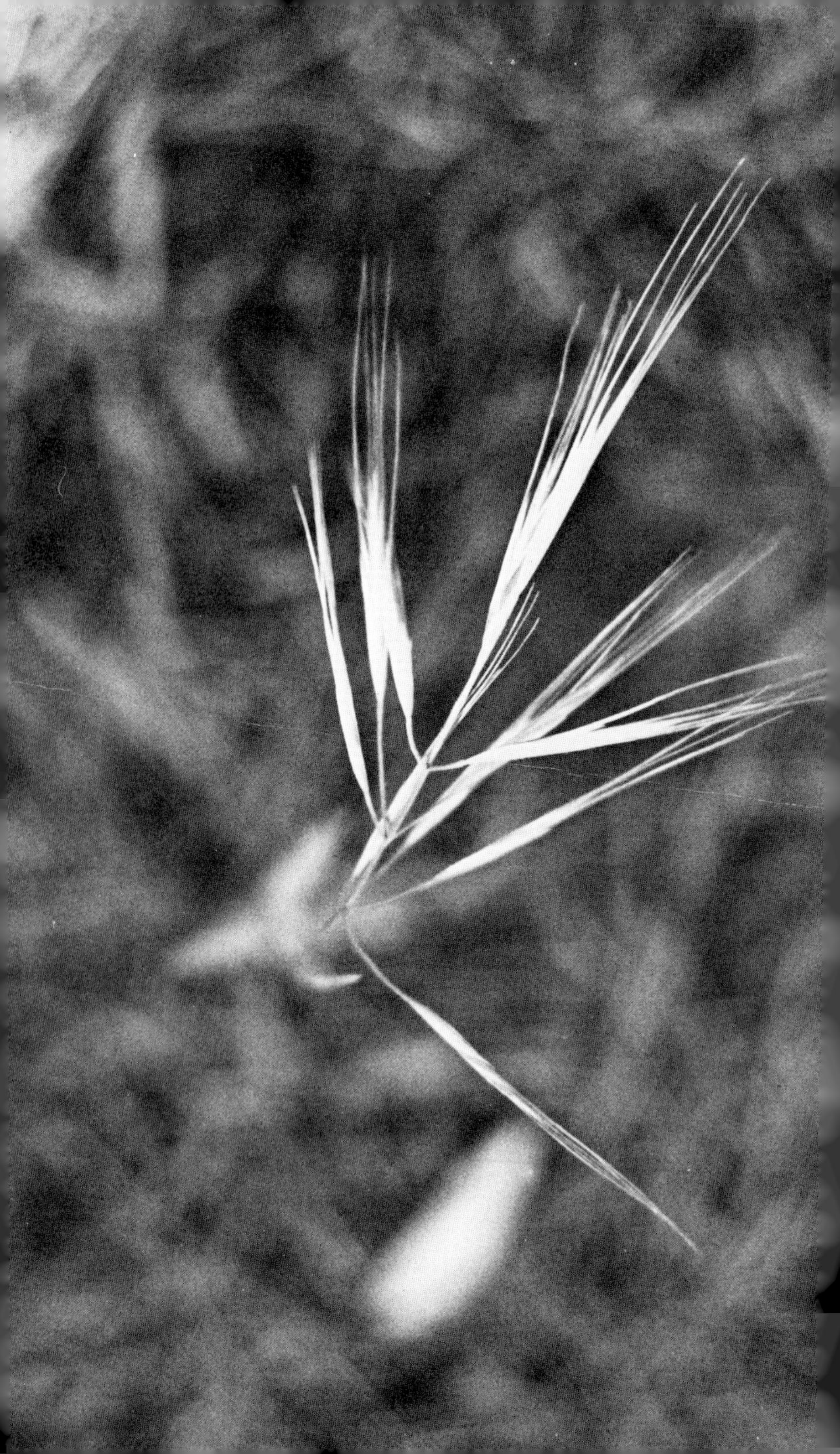

PRAYERS

We prayed more
   and received less.
We prayed to the early
   Christian kingdom,
We prayed for highways
   to replace the sand.
We prayed for Harlem and Rome,
We prayed for Africa to belong.
   And we were the ones
   without a home!
We prayed looking up at the
   robin's nest.
We prayed more
   and received less.

We prayed to Jesus, God, and Man
We prayed to the fatback
   in the frying pan.
We prayed to people
   who were well-dressed,
We prayed to the man
   to let us rest.
We prayed to the straight blonde
   hair on the Man's head.
We prayed for the Ku Klux Klan's
   Mama who was on her death bed.
We prayed, we prayed,
   as praying became a test.
We prayed more
   and recieved less.

We prayed for sun,
We prayed for rain,
We used boiled roots
    from a tree to kill our pain.
We prayed lying down,
We prayed standing up,
We prayed in school,
We prayed in church,
We prayed at home,
We even prayed alone.
We prayed, we prayed, we prayed
    until we became a pest
We prayed more
    and recieved less.
    Now let me confess
    Some of us ain't praying no more,
    So what you gonna do, huh?

OTHER BOOKS OF INTEREST FROM
CELESTIAL ARTS

THE ESSENCE OF ALAN WATTS. The basic philosophy of Alan Watts in nine illustrated volumes. Now available:
  GOD. 64 pages, paper, $3.95
  MEDITATION. 64 pages, paper, $3.95
  NOTHINGNESS. 64 pages, paper, $3.95
WILL I THINK OF YOU. Leonard Nimoy's warm and compelling sequel to You & I. 96 pages, paper, $3.95
THE HUMANNESS OF YOU, Vol. I & Vol. II. Walt Rinder's philosophy rendered in his own words and photographs. Each: 64 pages, paper, $2.95.
MY DEAREST FRIEND. The compassion and sensitivity that marked Walt Rinder's previous works are displayed again in this beautiful new volume. 64 pages, paper, $2.95.
ONLY ONE TODAY. Walt Rinder's widely acclaimed style is again apparent in this beautifully illustrated poem. 64 pages, paper, $2.95
THE HEALING MIND by Dr. Irving Oyle. A noted physician describes what is known about the mysterious ability of the mind to heal the body. 128 pages, cloth, $7.95; paper, $4.95.
I WANT TO BE USED not abused by Ed Branch. How to adapt to the demands of others and gain more pleasure from relationships. 80 pages, paper, $2.95.
INWARD JOURNEY Art and Psychotherapy For You by Margaret Keyes. A therapist demonstrates how anyone can use art as a healing device. 128 pages, paper, $4.95.
PLEASE TRUST ME by James Vaughan. A simple, illustrated book of poetry about the quality too often lacking in our experiences—Trust. 64 pages, paper, $2.95.
LOVE IS AN ATTITUDE. The world-famous book of poetry and photographs by Walter Rinder. 128 pages, cloth, $7.95; paper, $3.95.
THIS TIME CALLED LIFE. Poetry and photography by Walter Rinder. 160 pages, cloth, $7.95; paper, $3.95.
SPECTRUM OF LOVE. Walter Rinder's remarkable love poem with magnificently enhancing drawings by David Mitchell. 64 pages, cloth, $7.95; paper, $2.95.
GROWING TOGETHER. George and Donni Betts' poetry with photographs by Robert Scales. 128 pages, paper, $3.95.
VISIONS OF YOU. Poems by George Betts, with photographs by Robert Scales. 128 pages, paper, $3.95.
MY GIFT TO YOU. New poems by George Betts, with photographs by Robert Scales. 128 pages, paper, $3.95.
YOU & I. Leonard Nimoy, the distinguished actor, blends his poetry and photography into a beautiful love story. 128 pages, cloth, $7.95; paper, $3.95.
I AM. Concepts of awareness in poetic form by Michael Grinder. Illustrated in color by Chantal. 64 pages, paper, $2.95.
GAMES STUDENTS PLAY (And what to do about them.) A study of Transactional Analysis in schools, by Kenneth Ernst. 128 pages, cloth, $7.95; paper, $3.95.

COVER DESIGN by MAREK A. MAJEWSKI